D1121789

Wisdom With
Understanding
is Better
Than Rubies

Lurine Karon Greenberg
Fine Arts Collection

JERRY LEE LEWIS

LOST *and* FOUND

JERRY LEE LEWIS

LOST *and* FOUND

Joe Bonomo

continuum

2009

The Continuum International Publishing Group Inc
80 Maiden Lane, New York, NY 10038

The Continuum International Publishing Group Ltd
The Tower Building, 11 York Road, London SE1 7NX

www.continuumbooks.com

A catalog record for this book is available from the Library of
Congress.

ISBN 978 0 82642 966 7

Typeset by Pindar NZ, Auckland, New Zealand
Printed in the United States of America

CONTENTS

Acknowledgments.................................... ix

Photo Credits..................................... xiii

Lyric Credits......................................xv

Introduction 1

Lost...5

Found...53

Down the Line....................................125

Longing for Home.................................179

Sources..193

Index..201

For Amy

ego: that which is symbolized by the pronoun I; the conscious thinking subject . . .

(Also, humorously, "self."), *Oxford English Dictionary*

ACKNOWLEDGMENTS

I have lots of people to thank. I'm especially grateful to Peter Checksfield, Horst-Dieter Fischer and Graham Knight for offering me their expertise and encouragement, as well as access to their private collections, as I wrote this book. Peter Checksfield and Bob Montalto read early drafts, and their fact-checking was invaluable. James Akenson at the International Country Music Conference and Tennessee Tech University was helpful in putting me in touch with important people, and I'm thankful for his support and enthusiasm. Thanks also to Dave Alvin, Philip Casson, Jim Dickinson, John Doe, Trevor Duplock, Colin Escott, Chet Flippo, Johnnie Hamp, Pete Harris, John Hawken, Jim Heath, John Hills, Perk Kallin, Jerry Kennedy, Philip Lewis, Sigi Loch, Jon Langford, Ken Lundgren, Paul MacPhail, Bill C. Malone, Andrew McRae, Tony Papard, Bobby Reed, Shelby Singleton, Nick Warburton, and all of the enthusiastic, knowledgeable, and obliging folk at the Jerry Lee Lewis Unofficial Fan Forum and the Jerry Lee Lewis International Fan Club Yahoo Forum.

Thanks as well to my family and friends, and to the following people who generously provided material and/or moral support: James Bailey at Yep Roc Records, Jerry Bloom at More Black Than Purple, Paul Bonomo, Alan Clayson, Steve Coleman, Roger Cooper at The Nashville Teens, Kate Daniels at Vanderbilt University, Petra Deka, Glenn Dicker at Yep Roc Records, Salwa Elalwani at Tulane University, John E. Espinosa, Tom Merlino, and Shantel Burgess at Retna Ltd., Heide Fehrenbach at Northern Illinois University, Steve Fisher, Hans Frank, Randy Franklin at Yard Dog, Bill Harry, Bill Inglot, Ulf Krüger, Spencer Leigh, Jim "The Hound" Marshall, Louis McKelvey, Michael Montalto, Pierre Pennone, John Rauch at Rockstore, Bobby Reed, Dietrich Reusche at Museum für Moderne Kunst (Bremen), Marty Rogers, Siegfried Sander at Multiple Box, Roy Schonfeld at Abraham Associates, Gary Stewart, Wolfgang Thomas, Scott Weiss at Atomic Music Group, and Richard Weize at Bear Family.

Special thanks to Jon Langford for the front cover painting. Jon's artwork resides at the intersection of rock & roll spirit and vintage perpetuity, and I'm glad that he met me there.

At Northern Illinois University, thanks go to Dr. Katharina Barbe and her students in FLGE 484 Techniques of Translation II (Clare Blumenstein, Nyssa Bulkes, Heather Darsie, Lauren Hansen, Iska Hoerner, Travis Moore, Stevie Munz, Stefanie Piel, Kathrina Rainault, Taylor Reed, and Andrei Rosulescu). Additional thanks to Travis Moore. I'm grateful also to the hardworking staff at the Music Library and at the Interlibrary Loan Information Delivery Services at Founders Library.

David Barker at Continuum invited me to write this book, and was characteristically encouraging, open-minded, and supportive during its making. Thanks also to John Mark Boling, Katie Gallof, Max Novick, and Benn Linfield at Continuum, and to Kim Pillay and her colleagues at G.A. Pindar and Son NZ Ltd.

Above all, and again, thanks to Amy: loving, enthusiastic, smart, and a great reader. This book wouldn't be here without her.

PHOTO CREDITS

All photos of Jerry Lee Lewis: K&K. Permission by Retna LTD.

LYRIC CREDITS

INTRODUCTION

Sincerity has been with us as long as we've been with each other. The word first appeared in print in England in the middle of the sixteenth century, in reference to Christ's purity. Humans have dealt sincerely (and not) with each other since well before the Renaissance, but its toehold in language is relatively recent. The word derives from the Latin *sinceritas*, which originated from *sincerus*, meaning "sound, pure, whole"; linguists suggest that sincerus might have grown out of the idea of "one growth" — that is, not a hybrid or a mix. At its bedrock, sincerity means, simply and profoundly, that which emerges from that which is not falsified.

Blow off the dust, take a few long strides into the twenty-first century, and you get the truth — lived-in emotion. No bullshit.

Jerry Lee Lewis: Lost and Found is about sincerity. Jerry Lee's greatest music — which is not, as popular opinion holds, exclusive to his late 1950s recordings — is among the most passionately delivered and distinctive in popular music; his lesser is hollow, artificial, and rote. In this career there's a lot of treasure and a lot of garbage. In between is a story of rise and fall, and of the noise made at the intersection between art and commerce, and, a little further down the block, between integrity and insincerity. Because Jerry Lee is such an audacious original, his artistic highs are as dangerous as his lows. After I listened to hundreds of his songs scattered over a half-century's worth of albums, singles, and bootlegs, and after I deflected the tinny racket made by popular reconstructions and myths of the man, what I felt thrumming in his best work is sincerity: a pure sound, rock & roll and country, Gospel and Americana, that rises whole from its sources. When he was distracted — by whiskey, pills, producers, women, the *Billboard* charts, God, ego, Satan — Jerry Lee Lewis often gave rote performances, in the studio and on stage. When plugged in by part if not by all of the above, he often gave great, untouchable performances.

At the heart of this book is an extended exploration of *"Live" At The Star-Club*, the remarkable album that Jerry Lee Lewis recorded with the Nashville Teens in Hamburg, West Germany on April 5, 1964. It's one of the most honest and shockingly rocking albums ever made, by a man who many in his own homeland considered a stained and wicked has-been during a brutal passage in his career where he had to dig deep to find what moved him. I've conducted new interviews with members of the Nashville Teens, the album's producer Siggi Loch, and other musicians and fans who were at the show. Bookending my look at Hamburg and that album are historical overviews of how Jerry Lee got there and what he had to prove afterward. I cock my ear toward the sincerity of the recordings made before and after 1964, particularly his great Sun recordings of the late 1950s and his great country recordings of the late 1960s and early 1970s. Throughout, I come in and out of focus as a listener, both skeptical and converted.

Sincerity can be as stormy and elusive a foe as a friend. Jerry Lee Lewis' battles with it give shape to one of the great stories of popular culture.

LOST

The megalomaniac differs from the narcissist by the fact that he wishes to be powerful rather than charming, and seeks to be feared rather than loved. To this type belong many lunatics and most of the great men of history.

—Bertrand Russell

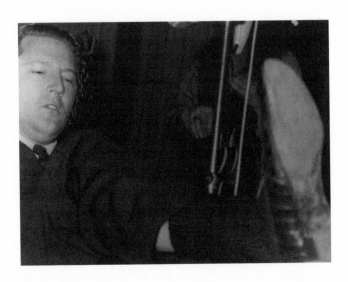

A blonde in a close-up smiles from an album jacket, wearing a football jersey, the number 20 stretched across her chest, her hair glowing, her teeth white and strong, her lips glistening, a wet tip of a tongue sneaking from the corner of her mouth. She was a flaxen model straight from central casting, but I didn't care how daunting or daring or original she wasn't. She was gorgeous. The family rec room in Wheaton, Maryland, the 1970s. I'm 11 or 12, sitting in a rocking chair in front of the stereo listening to a record that will soon pass into family lore.

The double-album remains indelible, and when I now gaze at the cover I feel something close to what I felt back then. The kicker was the back jacket. Remember now, I'm in sixth grade: the same model, composed in a medium shot, is still smiling flirtatiously, but her arms are frozen in the act of lifting her shirt, revealing a stomach shocking in its sudden whiteness. I'd stare at those teasing raised arms — the photo's placement on the back cover assured its semi-lewdness — and for long stretches dissolve into slack-jawed catatonia.

It didn't hurt that the girl looked a lot like Loretta Swit, who was then co-starring as "Hot Lips" Houlihan in *M*A*S*H* on Saturday nights, smacking her lips in the direction of Frank Burns while filling her uniform to bursting. I think that I pretended that it really was Swit on the album, and told lurid lies to that effect on the playground at St. Andrew the Apostle where I went to school. Nor did it hurt that her jersey was blue and gold, the same colors emblazoned on my older brothers' high school gym bags and book bags at Our Lady of Good Counsel High School, branding her as a denizen from an older world where girls spoke to men without shrieking or giggling, teasing out dates from them and maybe luring them into dimly lit bedrooms. (Remember, I'm in sixth grade.) Within a year I'd be peering at the adult pop album racks at Wheaton Public Library for a glimpse of the soft-core covers of Roxy Music's *Country Life* or Robert Palmer's *Pressure Drop*.

If the photos of my blonde siren seem corny and generic, they were. As intensely as that cover brings me back to the foaming days of adolescence, when I look at the softly tattered album now I feel the gloom of the whole enterprise. The production values are absurdly cheap: the girl is lit tackily, her shirt is chintzy and practically coming apart at the seams, her makeup is overdone, her hair Seventies-feathered. The album is *20 Rockin' Originals*, one of an endless line of shoddy compilation albums released on the Pickwick label that lined the racks at Korvettes, Dart Drug, and other chain discount department stores and supermarkets in the early and mid-1970s. My dad, or maybe one of my older brothers, bought the record for the family in 1974 or thereabouts, urged by smooth-talking Dick Clark to forget about Watergate, Vietnam, and the gas crisis (though Clark didn't use these words exactly) and to twist to the boppin' sounds of whitebread America where Chubby Checker and Dion will bring smiles to your anxious faces. The album compiled a hodge-podge of tracks from artists common to their vintage and commercial oblivion circa the F.M. radio era of the Eagles and Chicago. The Big Bopper, the Five Satins, Bill Haley & His Comets, Ray Stevens, whose outrageously un-P.C. masterpiece "Ahab the Arab" had my family in stitches nightly. "Two Platters!" promised the cover copy in sad un-hipness. The zero in "20" was a grainy photo of a vintage jukebox, a relic in the era of 8-track tapes, shag rugs, and quadraphonic sound. The same year that *20 Rockin'*

Originals was released, Pickwick issued the highly dubious album *The Beatles: 1962–1970* by Kings Road, a group of faceless studio musicians charged with recording cover versions of Beatles hits so astonishingly lame and dismal that my brothers and I could never listen without bursting out laughing. In the manner that kids can intuit desperation in grown-ups, we were nearly embarrassed for those musician hacks who, though they were simply earning a living, sounded and played *nothing* like the Beatles.

At least the songs on *20 Rockin' Originals* were, as the title guaranteed, originals — that is, performed by the original artists. Not yet hip to the swindle and cynicism of the cheapo compilation ethos, I listened to the record but didn't get that a handful of the songs were re-recordings of earlier hits. The tunes were fun. "Shake, Rattle & Roll," "Rockin' Robin," "Sh-Boom," and "Chantilly Lace" were irresistible to me and my brothers and sister. Privately I was beginning to cock my ear toward the melodramatic complications in songs like "The Great Pretender" and "I'll Remember (In The Still Of The Night)," and even the hangover vibe in the Champs' "Too Much Tequila." Wilbert Harrison's "Kansas City" was cool — I knew the Beatles' version from *Beatles '65* — and "Sheila" by Tommy Roe and Dusty Springfield's "I Only Want To Be With You" were simply great. But I think I knew somehow that Chuck Berry's "Reelin' and Rocking" and Charlie Ryan's "Hot Rod Lincoln" were lame remakes. For years the album made for great fun down in our rec room and basement as we laughed and danced around. Years later someone dropped the record and a small chip around the rim snapped off; to this day it's a symbol of the record's knockabout, well-worn fun.

One of the songs on the album bothered me: "Breathless,"
by Jerry Lee Lewis. By the mid-Seventies Lewis was com-
mencing a downturn from a mammoth second career in
music, having, since 1968, notched scores of hits on the
country charts and revitalized his dilapidated recording
livelihood, if not yet mastering marriage and sobriety. I
wouldn't have known any of this as a kid — country music
didn't much penetrate our split-level on Amherst Avenue
nor the homes of my friends, and my ears wouldn't
swivel toward Nashville for many years — so, while I was
listening to *20 Rockin' Originals*, Jerry Lee Lewis existed
as a much different icon to me: an old-timer, a has-been,
a weird graying guy who I vaguely associated with rolled
jeans and ducktails, girl trouble, a kind of tacky tawdri-
ness. He had little relevance to me, busy as I was awaiting
puberty, the next Wings album, and the latest lesson from
my brother on the significance of the words to "Stairway
To Heaven." Jerry Lee was strictly Fifties and strictly out
of it. I rolled my eyes. He would turn 40 in 1975 but to me
he already seemed old.

Culturally, I had a lot of help in this pigeonholing of
Lewis. George Lucas' *American Graffiti* opened in the summer of 1973, the same year that *20 Rockin' Originals* took
its humble place in the budget-racks, and would gross over
$21,000,000 in that year alone. By the time I was 10, *Happy
Days* had become the most popular sitcom on television,
gliding American culture comfortably and somewhat
inanely back to an era shot through with canned laughter.
Both the film and the ABC sitcom became instant cultural
artifacts, Zeitgeist barometers by which I would, in large
part, come to measure the decade. I was too young to go
see *American Graffiti* in the theaters in its premiere — I'm
sure that my brothers did, or I might've heard about it

from Rob T. or Billy P., my renegade buddies who were sneaking into the movies, or blessed with cool parents who let them into PG flicks. I'd eventually watch the movie on television as millions of other Americans would, and it renders the pre-disco/pre-punk Seventies as a time of affection for Fifties camp. Though *American Graffiti* was ostensibly set in 1962, it all looked like poodle skirts and teddy bears to me — and what did it matter when Suzanne Somers showed up in the convertible and smiled at the camera? It was the golden past. In 1978 *American Hot Wax* was released, and the Fifties were officially embalmed. As Greil Marcus writes in *The Dustbin of History*, "the movie version of the pop past shows only isolation." There was Jerry Lee, guilty by association, entombed in a past that he seemed destined to live out again and again, in perpetual isolation from the — from *my* — present.

The Fonz was much, much cooler than the Killer. He was younger, rode a motorcycle, was on television every Tuesday night, and had girls flocking to him wherever he walked. As anyone who was an adolescent in the Seventies will remember, the Fonz was undeniable: aloof, nice; tough, warm; street-smart with a shrouded history. Henry Winkler played him perfectly, with the right notes of cockiness and humor. When I learned later that Winkler was a trained dancer, it made sense, and didn't sissify Fonz at all for me; it only helped me to better appreciate the cool glide that was his weekly entrance. There were two things I especially loved about his character: the thumbs-up, and the magic fist. You remember the fist or, in another variation, the flat palm. No jukebox or pay phone stayed busted for long when the Fonz was around.

Happy Days was initially one of three playlets featured

on a *Love, American Style* television episode from 1973. Surprised but thrilled ABC executives discovered that its boldly innocent, fraudulently fond "look back" at the fraudulently innocent 1950s was just what Americans mired in Vietnam and lingering at the precipice of Watergate wanted, indeed craved. *Happy Days* premiered in early 1974 and, wildly popular at its mid-Seventies peak, ran for ten seasons. I was a huge fan, and my younger brother and I went so far as to share a clandestine Cool Religion whose dogma involved the solemn laying-on of a "thumbs-up" sign. (The sooner I forget about this, the better.) For all we knew, "Al's" was one of a million such diners in the United States in the Fifties, where everything gleamed and any problem worked itself out amidst laughter in 23 minutes. *Racism* might simply have been a dirty word scrawled in the bathroom stall. We knew nothing of the con: we watched, girls swooned, Nielsen ratings soared, I punched our kitchen radio with my fist when no one was around hoping that the Top 40 might fill the room.

At St. Andrew the Apostle we had "Fifties Day," when the teaching nuns and lay faculty encouraged us to show up to school dressed as our favorite icon of that beloved decade. The last thing I wanted to do was call more attention to my skinny, acne-menaced physique and emotional complications so I and several other kids merely skulked onto the playground in jeans and white t-shirts, desperate for invisibility, maybe a couple of us daring to roll up our jeans. But Donald M. (for whom the role "teacher's pet" was coined) strutted into school in full Fonz regalia, complete with Mom-assisted greased-back hair, leather jacket and black boots, the costume wrapping snugly around his chubby body. Alas, the inevitable comeuppance: when sassy, large-breasted Wendy R. cruelly waltzed over to him in front of the gallery of popular kids and crooned "Donny Angel" at him, poor Donald's face burned amidst the scornful laughter.

What became of *Happy Days*? It was destined for a ratings plunge, a dip into "serious" issues, the departure of its lead stars, and, finally, cancellation. The sitcom suspended certain cultural artifacts in time, allowing the vitality to drain off. Frowning on *American Graffiti* — which *Happy Days* was expressly created to cash in on — Marcus writes that "the boys and girls of [that film] were kept so busy turning themselves into pop myths, or just keeping up with the pop myths Lucas bought into long ago, that they never had time to feel out their roles, play with their faces, or bounce self-pity off narcissism — that last being my idea of what High School U.S.A. was all about."

Back to "Breathless." In the rec room, listening to *20 Rockin' Originals*, I felt that something was off. I'm fascinated now at my adolescent intuition: an instinct, a glimmer, a feeling that the song I was (literally) rocking to was phony, wasn't "tough," as I might've said a couple of years earlier. Part of this was due to the obvious, if false, nostalgia cast by the album and artwork. Had I heard the original Sun Records recording from January of 1958 yet? I don't think I could have. No one in my family had any Jerry Lee Lewis records, let alone any from his Sun era, and certainly none of my classmates did. It's possible that I'd heard the song on the radio, though I don't recall a specific memory nor how prevalent oldies radio stations might have been in the Washington, D.C. area in the mid-Seventies. Just as likely I *hadn't* heard the original song, and my introduction to "Breathless" and to Jerry Lee Lewis came with *20 Rockin'*

Originals. An affectionate overture to be sure, but a flawed one. And many years too late.

What I'd greeted was a myth, but I'd missed the artist. Jerry Lee Lewis had re-recorded "Breathless" on September 24, 1963 in Nashville with producers Jerry Kennedy and Shelby Singleton. At the end of that decade Singleton would acquire from Sam Phillips the Sun Records recording masters and inadvertently open up a treasure trove of unreleased gems, including dozens of unheard Lewis recordings. But in 1963 Lewis was a long way from that happy accident, which would dovetail with his emergence as a popular country music artist, and from those original late Fifties/early Sixties Sun recording sessions. In between, Lewis would find himself around the world battling down an endless road of semi-full club dates, punctuated with a handful of singles and albums each disappearing quicker from the charts than the one before. In taking over the helm of Lewis' recording career at Smash, the affiliate label of parent-company Mercury to which Lewis had singed a contract in September, Singleton had a plan for the troubled 28 year old, born as much from crass commercial consideration as from artistic sympathy. "The first thing I did with acts that I signed in those years who had had hit records is I immediately went into the studio and I cut a greatest hits album," Singleton explained to Colin Escott. "That way, because of the lack of the availability of the other product in the marketplace, a greatest hits album would recoup whatever advance I gave him, plus it gave me working capital to work on the new product." Listening somewhat skeptically to "Breathless" a decade later, I was too young to understand or much care about *product in the marketplace, advance, working capital.* All I knew was that I felt ripped-off listening to a song that sounded hollow, forced, a relic from a mummified era. Lewis himself might have felt unfulfilled, re-cutting the very songs that several years earlier had branded him as an iconoclastic, break-the-mold hell-raiser.

When Lewis signed with Mercury Records he was, commercially-speaking, a phantom. Always the embodied promise of mayhem and thrills onstage, Lewis was suffering mightily on the *Billboard* charts, and hadn't scored a hit since 1961's "What'd I Say," which had peaked at 30 on the Pop Singles chart. He'd had some success recently on the country charts where three of his flip sides — "You Win Again," "I'll Make It All Up To You," and "Cold, Cold Heart" — had charted high, but that wasn't where the stardom was for Lewis. As the mid-Sixties approached, he was chubby and dismayed, hunched over the piano in Sam Phillips' studio at 639 Madison Avenue in Memphis, the longest-tenured artist there, filtering the great American songbook through manic fingers and bravado, enduring the gloss of orchestral strings and female back-up singers while competing with Nashville, glaring through red-shot bourbon eyes at the ascendancy of seemingly every rock and pop singer but himself. He was heading for the daze of oblivion rather than the daze brought on by whiskey or feral women. The Killer was invisible. There can't be a worse curse thrown at a giant ego.

By now it's an old tale, as indelible as Juliet on the balcony or Paul Bunyan in the forest, bearing in this case the imagery of trashy Southern culture, a sinning young man, and the myth of the rise-and-fall. Most fans will know about Jerry Lee Lewis' fateful week in May of 1958 — should I resist retelling the story? By the time I'd first listened to Lewis, the scandal of his wedding at age

23 to his 13-year-old second-cousin Myra Brown had already and permanently rewritten the narrative. He was the young, lecherous hepcat from way down south who shrugged his shoulders at incest and couldn't keep his sweaty hands off the jailbait. The black-and-white photos were unforgettable: Lewis in his sharp Fifties suit and slicked-back hair, smirking happily (knowingly), his arm around a girl who looked like she was about nine years old. She was cute, in an Eisenhower-era way, and she looked frightened and giddy and brave — she was a young girl. And the guy sitting next to her was going to get his hand up her skirt that night (and probably already had) but he was a blood relative and that was what mattered. Or so it felt to me looking at the photos in *Time* magazine. And likely it will always feel that way to those who experience Lewis' career by navigating the imagery and nomenclature that popular culture makes official, or to those who limit themselves to stories set in stone.

But Lewis had to keep moving. His shock and dismay at the uproar — initially in England at the cusp of an important tour, soon after in America — was entirely genuine; he really didn't understand the scope of the outrage directed at him by a world that only two weeks ago was bathing him in adulation, packed clubs, and $10,000 paydays. That's the story and the myth, and that's also the truth.

Lewis had met Myra through his bass player and Tennessee cousin J.W. Brown, ten years his senior. Myra was Brown's daughter, and Lewis' eyes went straight through her. I don't need to belabor the leering pull of lust, but for Lewis the growing attraction for Myra was more than simple hunger in that it was affection couched in cultural norms — doused in Lewis' crotch-worship, yes, but setting sturdily upon bedrock Southern permissiveness. Brown had been a telephone-wire repairman in Memphis, but he was souring on the job. His luck in avoiding electrical shocks was long and happy, but the highest-watt jolt couldn't have roused him from the ennui he was suffering making a living for his wife and daughter while ignoring the siren-call of music, his love since he was a teenager.

As ironic luck would have it, Brown was injured on the job, and he took that as a sign. He knew that his cousin Jerry Lee, late of Southwestern Assemblies of God University in Waxahachie, Texas where he'd stirred up trouble letting his fingers do the talking, was playing piano and kicking up some noise down in Louisiana. So he cashed in a year's worker's compensation, made the five-hour drive down Interstate 55 to Natchez, and tried to talk Lewis into coming back up to Memphis with him to start a knockabout band. Lewis declined, hedging his bets playing piano weekly at the Wagon Wheel nightclub in Natchez, flirting skirts and waiting for Sam Phillips — for anyone, really — to call him back with a record deal and bags of money, his fate delivered at last.

But a few days later, Lewis was in Memphis. Always itching to get somewhere and do something, Lewis decided to take Brown up on the offer, and on a Sunday night in October 1956 called his surprised cousin from a drugstore payphone. As Myra remembers it, Lewis strolled into the house that night wearing cowboy boots and a fresh haircut. Where was she? At the dining room table finishing her homework. She was 12, Lewis was 21. Many myths begin quietly: shy Myra thought that cocky Jerry Lee was cute; Jerry Lee flirted; Myra's dad warned her that her cousin was a married man.

Three takes on those first blushing weeks. In careful and distancing third-person, Myra writes of the evening she met Lewis:

> For the first meeting . . . something more dramatic than homework, dinner, and a brief piano recital was called for, yet the quickest sight could not penetrate the deep thoughts behind seemingly innocent glances. If it is possible for love at first sight to exist without the participants realizing it in so many words, then that was the very case with Myra and Jerry. At the dinner table, Jerry was allowed several minutes to gaze at Myra unrestricted by shyness and modesty. His gimlet eyes gravitated toward her face, plain and unpainted but commonly handsome. He became detached from his identity as her cousin and looked at her beyond the barriers of family. He saw an attractive girl, who she was and what she was and her tender years made no difference. Myra regarded Jerry in the same unattached manner. As cousins, second cousins to be exact, she was permitted to love him by virtue of their kinship. The preliminary matter of learning to like the stranger was overcome the moment he stepped in the front door. He was a man in the pride and prime of his life. She was an innocent child. He was worldly-wise; she, a clean slate.

Delete the orchestral strings from the soundtrack, and here's Frankie Jean, Lewis' younger sister:

> Jerry had been staying with Myra's family in

Memphis for about a year. Jerry was very easily enticed by women and they'd leave this 13-year-old girl in the house wearing these skimpy little pyjamas.

Then, there's Jerry:

Myra and me, we got together in the back seat of my car. I knew she wasn't a virgin. I must be the onliest man in the world that married his 13-year-old cousin and she wasn't a virgin, can you believe that? Momma pleaded with me not to marry her. But I wanted her and I'm a stubborn mother-humper.

Besides, I loved Myra.

From the sacred to the profane. So many tendrils reach back to Lewis' marriage that they are hopelessly entangled, truths coiling around myths until they've become impossible to distinguish, except that together they bloom to make a great story. The facts are plain: ages, dates on marriage licenses, documented court appearances, mug shots, prescription pads, gigs played club after club, songs recorded take after take. But the story of Jerry Lee Lewis is so large, so fraught with legend and folklore, that facts often will wilt under the harsh and sexy glare of mystique.

Yet the facts of Jerry Lee Lewis' marriage to his cousin will be repeated heedless of accuracy or ethics, seduced by our human tendency toward romanticizing and sensationalizing the past in order to get us off in the present. And in the present we have received the life of the Killer in three eras: *Sun*; *Scandal*; *Comeback*. Wish as we might to rub away the lurid from the prosaic, the truth remains that the career of Jerry Lee Lewis long ago entered the hands of story-tellers and myth-makers beyond his control. That's the way we want it. And, to a certain degree, that's the way it happened. And that's why the tale has been spun so often, from backstage to Hollywood to the local bar. Lewis' marriage to Myra was the beginning of the end. But the end never really came.

On November 1, 1957 Sun Records issued Jerry Lee Lewis' single "Great Balls Of Fire" backed with "You Win Again." Three months later, on the first day in February, Sun issued his next single, "Breathless" backed with "Down The Line." In between those releases, on December 12, 1957, Jerry Lee married Myra Brown in Hernando, Mississippi, at a popular, hush-hush eloping spot.

Myra was adjusting to being Mrs. Lewis — a baffling, overwhelming adjustment that involved attending grade school while filling a new house with furniture, learning to drive in a brand-new red Cadillac, and cocking one timid ear to the complaints of Jane, Jerry Lee's second wife and mother of his two sons and a woman to whom he was still married, and the other blushing ear to the increasing pants and squeals of the knocked-out girls at Jerry Lee's shows. The Killer was on the road, basking in growing paydays, raucous audiences, and adulation of those wet-mouthed, underwear-loosed young women availing themselves of this shocking, incredibly sexy bad boy of rock & roll. Jerry Lee was always on the road, hocking his singles, satisfying Sam Phillips' bottom-line, shouting, loving his music, slamming his piano keys night after night, testifying, letting Jesus and Satan wrestle it out as he championed the scrum and blurred the absurdity with bourbon and self-protective bravado.

He already had two singles — "Crazy Arms," his auspicious debut, and "Whole Lotta Shakin' Goin' On" — and an EP (*The Great Ball Of Fire*) behind him, and they were hot. "Crazy Arms" would sell a quarter million copies through its first year, and "Whole Lotta Shakin' Goin' On" — in many ways the quintessential Killer record — would become the largest selling Sun single in history, millions of copies bought and spun, landing the record at the top of the pop, country, and rhythm & blues charts by the end of 1957. At the time of his marriage to Myra, Jerry Lee had appeared three times on *The Steve Allen Show* — the second appearance featuring the iconic rock & roll moment when Allen threw Jerry Lee's piano bench across the stage after Lewis had launched it out from under himself, an hysterical instant where the studio and television audiences could feel the cultural grounds shifting beneath them. "I love quality, and Jerry Lee sure had it," marveled Allen. "The response was incredible, we had him back and he blew away everyone's viewing figures, including Ed Sullivan's. Jerry Lee was a star from then on."

There would be three appearances on *American Bandstand*, and one on Alan Freed's *Big Beat Party* (Jerry Lee: "Without Alan Freed back in those days you had nothin' . . . you were pissing into the wind.") These were the idol-making media splashes that cemented Lewis' career: the striped shirts; the cocky shoes; the ten-inch mop of blond hair falling in his face as he'd stand at the piano and pound and holler; his band behind him grinning and struggling to keep up; Dick Clark's friendship and professional support. And the girls. "By 1958 Jerry Lee Lewis was on top," writes Nick Tosches. "Of all the rock & roll creatures, he projected the most hellish persona. He was feared more than the rest, and hated more too.

Preachers railed against him, mothers smelled his awful presence in the laundry of their daughters, and young boys coveted his wicked, wicked ways."

And the road always called, would always call for Jerry Lee. The weeks leading up to his fateful outing in England in the spring of 1958 were typically full and, at this point in his heady, young career, typically successful. A mere 11 days after marrying Myra he was in New York City co-headlining a 12-day residency at the Paramount Theater with Fats Domino, demolishing previous attendance records, playing dozens of shows before thousands of stomping fans. Back home in the new year for a bit of rest and play-acting as dutiful husband at 4752 Dianne Drive in Memphis (a ten-minute drive from Elvis' Graceland), Lewis was soon back in the bus, trusting his driver to safely steer him and his backing trio to the next series of gigs.

January saw Lewis play Georgia, Louisiana, and Virginia, where Jerry Lee had a run-in with a lame piano. "To me a piano is like a lady," Jerry Lee wrote in his autobiography. "You have to show it who's boss. I was playing Yorktown [Virginia], one time, and the piano they'd set up for me was a big old baby grand and it didn't have too many notes workin' on it. I started playing it and I said, 'Jesus, this is ridiculous,' and I got real mad and started kicking it, 'cause I'm a pretty serious person when it comes to my piano. I kicked it out of the club, down the sidewalk, and I kicked it into the ocean. I swear to God this is true! I think they set me up with this piano as a joke but the joke was on them when the thing sunk in the ocean. The audience followed me along the dock." The Killer believes the tale.

After a quick one-off gig at the Rancho Club in Riverside, California, the fellas were off to Hawaii for a sold-out show at the Civic Auditorium in Honolulu, and then a long flight over the Pacific for an Australian tour. (Did Jerry Lee cast his gaze out the window and look for his soaked piano below?) Jerry Lee rocked Sydney, Newcastle, Brisbane, and Melbourne in a whirlwind week, plus another show in Honolulu on the long way back. As his plane landed in Memphis, "Breathless" was ascending the charts. Jerry Lee could see his name written in the constellations above him. The shadow of his increasingly rancorous divorce from Jane was leaning gloomily (and ominously) over his personal life, but Jerry Lee was so heady with his rapid success that he barely noticed.

In addition to another appearance on March 18 on *American Bandstand* — now swimming in good will with Sun Records due to a Beechnut Gum promotion that was moving thousands of copies of "Breathless" — Jerry Lee continued his vault into popular consciousness via Freed's *Big Beat Show*, an ambitious three-month revue featuring Buddy Holly, Larry Williams, The Chantels, Screamin' Jay Hawkins, Chuck Berry (who famously feuded with Jerry Lee, though many of the accounts of hostility and racism, recorded elsewhere, remain unverified), and others. The six-hour show opened at the Paramount Theater in Brooklyn, swung though Manhattan and the Bronx, Connecticut, Philadelphia, Baltimore, Dayton, Grand Rapids, Cleveland, Canton, and Columbus, Ohio, up into Ontario, Canada, back down to Ohio, Michigan, St. Louis, Tulsa, Oklahoma, Wichita, Kansas, Kansas City, Missouri, Nebraska, Chicago . . . The tour was exhaustive and exhausting, and Jerry Lee's manic stage show was an indelible reminder of the ferocious talent hardwired into the kid from Ferriday. Rock & roll, earmarked by Freed as

American teenagers' holy writ, right, and privilege, was igniting sparks in bedrooms and dens across the county, and those sparks were catching flame in the concerns of parents, social conservatives, religious leaders, and just about anyone over the age of 25 who considered himself law-abiding.

Freed shrewdly capitalized on these tensions. The *Big Beat* became a notorious public spectacle, culminating at the May 3 show in Boston. Chuck Berry was headlining on this night, and during Jerry Lee's performance the Boston police, already concerned from reports of unruly, dancing patrons at other cities, interrupted the show and asked the promoters to lower the noise. Jerry Lee insisted on finishing his show, but during Berry's performance, after Freed infamously incited the crowd by claiming over the PA that "The police don't want teenagers to have any fun!", some patrons began throwing chairs, cops intervened, and a small-scale riot erupted (though its size and consequences have been exaggerated over the years). The unhappy evening made the headlines, and though several of the remaining shows went on without incident, the Troy, Providence, New Haven, and Newark shows were cancelled. Freed was eventually charged by a Massachusetts grand jury for inciting unlawful destruction. Though the payola scandal that would prove to be Freed's ruin was a few years away, the whiff of shame and dishonor must've been in the air. Jerry Lee would face his own calamitous disgrace within the month.

Happy news prevailed for the time being. The *Big Beat* controversy had touched off even more flames around Jerry Lee, and he'd been in and out of the Sun studio for months bringing smoldering fingers to his considerable store of tunes. Sun issued his new single two days before

the Boston show: "High School Confidential" was promoted via the Mamie Van Doren-graced B-movie of the
same name. The Killer's magic was potent; the 45 broke
the Top 20 on the Pop charts while the flip side, "Fools
Like Me," was a Top 10 country chart hit. A couple of
weeks later, Sun issued Jerry Lee's first full-length, a self-
titled album comprised of his recent singles filled out with
lively and wholly original studio sides.

On May 17, a beautiful spring Saturday, the town of
Ferriday celebrated "Jerry Lee Lewis Day," complete with
the Ferriday High School marching band, a parade of fan
club members with Jerry Lee in his open-top convertible
as center display, the bestowing of the key to the city
and commemorative plaque by Mayor W.D. Davis, and
an appearance in front of the Senior Class at Ferriday
High. All very squeaky-clean, civic-pride stuff: Jerry Lee
would bask in the high sun, Myra at his side, record sales
climbing, the din and excitement of the *Big Beat* show
and packed club-dates ringing in his ears, studio sessions
lined up, songwriters begging for attention. Elvis had just
had his long hair shorn and been inducted into the U.S.
Army. Ferriday and Memphis could wait a while. The rest
of the world needed conquering, and England was calling
for the Killer.

"I'm Myra, Jerry's wife." Anyone with a casual knowledge
of Jerry Lee Lewis knows two facts about the man: he married his underage cousin, and the marriage derailed his
career. Many also know that he resurrected said career on
the country charts at the end of the 1960s. What the casual
fan may want to know is what happened in between: the
dwindling paydays, the scattered crowds at diminishing
clubs, and the songs.

The U.K. tour was a catastrophe. The press conference at the Westbury Hotel in Mayfair, where Jerry Lee, Myra, and the entourage were staying, was preserved in flashbulb infamy and wired around the world to be stamped among the century's emblematic pop-culture touchstones. When news spread that the crazy Southern cat had married his teenage cousin while still married to his second wife, and that he was grinning and (cockily?) answering every question put to him as if he had the birthright to inbreed — the outrage soon followed. Although some of the following decade's calamities supposedly suffered by Jerry Lee professionally and personally have been exaggerated down the years, it appears that very little of the marriage scandal has been embellished: Jerry Lee was indeed targeted by Fleet Street, swiftly and efficiently, and the tour in London and outlying towns was shaken unmercifully and permanently. Within hours he was playing to semi-full clubs and theatres, enduring hoots and slurs lobbed at him by patrons believing, semi-seriously or not, indignantly or with a half-grin, that the Killer was a weirdo cradle-snatcher. "Think how we must have felt back in 1958 as the hillbilly courting behaviour of some citizens of America's Deep South unfolded in our newspapers," writes Ray Connolly in a *Daily Mail* article a half-century after the scandal. "We'd heard about the phenomenon of the child bride in fiction from the Tennessee Williams' play and the film *Baby Doll*. But buttoned-up, respectable, repressed Fifties Britain had never come across the real thing before. With Jerry Lee, the Louisiana swamps had exceeded all expectations in what they had thrown up.

"Were this to happen today," Connolly continued, "any star would instantly surround himself with a legion of publicists who would do their utmost to put a positive gloss on the situation — not the easiest of tasks, I have to admit. Come to think of it, just about impossible. But those were less sophisticated times when it came to media manipulation." The tour was cancelled ignominiously on May 26, two days after it had started. In the span of 48 hours, Jerry Lee Lewis had passed a critical and fateful threshold: from young star to crippled disgrace. The issue sparked fiery editorials in British papers and in corner pubs, prompted the police to investigate the legality of the marriage and the potential criminality of Jerry Lee's very presence in the country. The marriage was even debated in the House of Commons. In West Virginia, the *Morgantown Post* was more than pleased to run a frowning commentary reprinted from London's *Daily Express*: "The verdict of Britain's teen-agers on Jerry Lee Lewis' matrimonial entanglements was clear and unhesitating. So Jerry Lee Lewis is back in the United States. The young rock and rollers of Britain are oft accused of being unbalanced and of giving way to their emotions too freely. But in this instance they have shown a sure, mature judgment that is much to their credit. Young idols of the guitar and the microphone are raised to great heights in popular esteem in a very few weeks. But they are learning that it takes even less time for them to fall."

Greil Marcus wrote that Jerry Lee Lewis represented "all the mythical strangeness of the redneck south: lynch-mob blood-lust, populist frenzies, even incest."

Shrugged Jerry Lee: "I was a 21-year-old kid, and I didn't know whether I was comin' or goin'. We were just kids in love at the time. It didn't matter to me. I was getting to sell more records than Elvis. He had gone into the army and I was hitting big, but there were a lot of narrow-

minded people who thought I was corrupting the youth.
I'd figured out my style, I done it my way and I was very
hard-headed."

Myra would remark later, "Here was a man made for
people to hate." For Jerry Lee, nothing would again be
the same.

Back in the States, Sam Phillips and Sun Records surveyed
the damage. All involved were fairly certain that the scorn
would evaporate once it reached American shores, that
Jerry Lee's recent chart and concert track record would
mightily pull him up and over any controversy he might
face in America.

Phillips' first gambit was, oddly, to release a novelty
single in an attempt both to reestablish Jerry Lee's clout
on the record charts and to smilingly shrug off the scandal
of his and Myra's marriage (which was under the radar
in America). "The Return Of Jerry Lee" was very much
a product of its era, and a great curiosity, as wholesome
as it was woefully misguided: made in the form of a
mock-interview, no doubt attempting to laugh away the
U.K. press conference, the single used snippets of Jerry
Lee's recent hit songs as "answers" to "questions" fired at
him from one "Edward R. Edward" from the "Municipal
Airport in Memphis, Tennessee, where Jerry Lee Lewis
and his bride have just returned from a tour of the British
Isles." Cobbled together on-the-fly in one day by Sun
producer Jack Clement and local dj George Klein, the
record, in addition to innocuous questions sending up
conservative Britons, the English press, and a red-faced
Queen Elizabeth, asks Jerry Lee if he might wish to say
something about his new lovely wife? Cue Jerry Lee's
lascivious growl from "Whole Lotta Shaking Going On."

Not especially wise publicity for a young man tarred with the tacky feathers of a letch.

As far as Jerry Lee's career was concerned, the idea should have remained in the theoretical stage, or at least in-house as a joke or tucked away on a 45 flip side and preferably not so soon after the English disaster (the record was released on June 1, less than a week after Jerry Lee returned, shaken, to the States). Sun promoted the record feebly, declining to mail out promo copies to dj's, and without radio support, head-on in the gale of the controversy, it stiffed. Thus began a long commercial decline.

Of far greater interest to history, and an indicator of the indefatigable Killer nature, was the b-side to "The Return Of Jerry Lee." A year earlier, Jerry Lee had been in the Sun studio laying tracks, working up masters and one-off's for his next single and the bulk of what would become his debut long-player. As was his tendency, and in a great and consistent display of his talent and knowledge of music history, Jerry Lee burned through a lot of tracks in these sessions, including "Old Time Religion," "When The Saints Go Marching In," "Love Letters In The Sand," "Pumpin' Piano Rock," and "Drinkin' Wine Spo-Dee-O-Dee," a pretty fair indication of the man's tension-filled, shape-shifting desires.

Among the tracks cut was an audacious, funny, cocky number called "Lewis Boogie," penned by Jerry Lee himself. The song begins, like so much great rock & roll, recklessly: an octave-by-octave tumble down the keyboard — "Hang on!" Jerry Lee yelps — gamely caught by Jimmy Van Eaton's rushed drum fill, guitarist Roland Janes catching up behind him. Jerry Lee grabs the mike, introduces himself and his proud home state, and promises a back-breaking good time. He sings simply and effortlessly and with great bravado, outlining in a few seconds in a small corner studio the terms of his gift, his vision, and his checkered career. As is the case with Jerry Lee's great early Sun recordings, Van Eaton and Janes don't so much accompany Jerry Lee as they come along for the ride — the rhythm track swings beautifully, and Van Eaton's and Janes' participation is crucial to the sound and vibe of the tune, much in the way that the shotgun-rider and backseat clowns are crucial for any drunken joyride.

Grinning, Jerry Lee continues the filthy decree/come-on, naming the damn thing and trademarking it, too. Satisfied that he's appointed the rules, he lays down a classic trademark solo, his fingers moving and darting between the song's simple changes, a wily fox eluding its captors. A few bars later and he's back to the geography lesson, this time hollering down the charms of bop and hot New Orleans. Janes takes a solo beneath Jerry Lee's hoots before the third verse, the kicker and brief window into the Killer's attitude: he slyly suggests a roadtrip down to Memphis to meet a certain boy who's called you nothin' but a hound. Who knows what will happen when we get there? Jerry Lee didn't have to worry about local retaliation — Elvis' Memphis mafia wasn't up to speed yet — but his boastfulness would be well known by anyone within earshot of the River City. Taking on Elvis wasn't a challenge for Jerry Lee: it was in his DNA. It was all done tongue firmly in cheek — Jerry Lee's having fun and making it fun, too. The track's over in two minutes and he's barely even worked up a sweat.

The song stayed on the shelf in Sun, as did literally hundreds of tracks that Jerry Lee cut in the late Fifties, most slowly but eventually released on various compilations in the following decades. But "Lewis Boogie" wasn't in limbo for too long: desperate, with money-tills clanking in his head, Phillips searched through the boxes of recorded tracks for an appropriate flip side to "The Return Of Jerry Lee" and found this, a far more native and instinctive response to the world's growing disgust with Jerry Lee Lewis than a self-parodying, defensive mock-interview on some imagined Southern tarmac.

"Lewis Boogie" was nothing short of Jerry Lee's calling card, his ID. His genetic map. "I'd figured out my style, I done it my way and I was very hard-headed."

No one heard it. "The Return Of Jerry Lee" was destined to remain obscure, but the singer had bigger problems, troubles wearing professional and personal scowls. Jerry Lee's demons will always dog him, and likely grew in passion and nature after the marriage scandal, and he'd spend the rest of his life managing them, subduing them, blurring them, fighting them, loving them. Rock & roll was the devil's music. The Killer felt that at heart and truly believed it — after his intense Pentecostal rearing and the Fall of Man — but he also felt and believed the music's power to be sexual, joyous, *and* redemptive. This would become the epic struggle of his personal life littered with wives, ex-wives, arrests, anonymous hotel groupies, heartbreaking deaths, pills and cocaine, booze, guns, and general meanness.

"Jerry is very spiritual," Phillips once told critic Robert Palmer, in an insightful observation. "Of course, I don't agree with the way he feels about the Bible and the here-after and everything, but that certainly is his prerogative. But it's also his frustration. He's very close to God, and yet he's very vain. And he is trying his best, and has all along, to get into trouble. He's a man of great, contrite heart who's just maybe messed himself up from time to time. He seems to have an affinity for walking into traps. You know, he's such an *extremely* talented human being. I'm not talking about voice, piano, any *one* thing. The guy has a photographic memory. He has an instinctive quality of relating to every damn type of song that you can think of, from pop to the lowest black blues. It's a shame he doesn't have anyone to direct his talent — he is one of the century's great, great talents. But he feels a lonesomeness in his talent, *extreme* lonesomeness for somebody to be strong around him."

Celebrate it, mythologize it, roll your eyes at it, condemn it — it's Jerry Lee's thorny bed of choices. His professional life after the spring of 1958 was new to him. Even if his ascendance had been brief, it had been incendiary and real, built on raw talent and hysterical self-confidence. When the gigs dried up, when the paydays dropped from thousands of drink- and Cadillac-buying dollars to a few hundred bucks split among too many musicians and hangers-on, when the hit singles vanished, when it appeared that Phillips and Sun Records were letting him wither on the vine but wouldn't cut down the vine if it might yet bloom down the road, it stung. The late 1950s and the bulk of the 1960s would become a fascinating display of how Jerry Lee's unbridled flair and oversized personality would be challenged in the face of industry indifference, cultural revulsion, has-been commercial status, and public and private disappointments. As Jerry Lee's personal life would face chaotic joy and tragedy in the coming years, so would his professional career face galling resistance and distress. Born with song and rhythm in his blood, he had little choice but to trust his revolving door of managers, duck every few months into the studio with the great American songbook, and set fire to theaters at night in whatever town would have him and his band. Soldier on, prove that rock & roll, finally, is what matters.

The big media guns — Dick Clark, in particular — were frightened by angry advertisers who were turning nervous ears to the concerns of parents, educators, and religious leaders who were troubled by the indelicate nature of Jerry Lee. Because Clark, and to a lesser extent Steve Allen and Alan Freed, were hesitant to book Jerry Lee on television, his appearances petered out. His troubles continued with the American Federation of Musicians. After the English debacle, Jerry Lee cancelled many American shows in addition to the U.K. performances, the unhappy beginning of an erratic tendency on his part to refuse to show up and play a contracted show if he felt that the promotion had been sketchy or that too few patrons had bought tickets. These "no-shows" did not sit well with booking agents and promoters, who had rented auditoriums and halls and guaranteed shows. The Musicians Union thus stopped paying his royalties from record sales until he in some measure paid back the angry promoters. The enmity between Jerry Lee and the Musicians Union would last for years, with missed shows and subsequent mounting fees, and without firm union backing Jerry Lee and his managers found it increasingly difficult to secure shows at larger venues.

Myra Lewis relates two sorry tales of road-woes that dramatize Jerry Lee's looming commercial oblivion in the late 1950s. In March of 1959, traveling with Myra, the band drove over a thousand miles through Texas, in the process missing a show in Dallas (much to the grudge-holding ire of the club owner), only to arrive at midnight for a late show in Albuquerque, New Mexico and discover that they'd missed their destination by some 300 miles. Two flat tires, a busted battery, and junky air-conditioning in the car didn't help the tense matters. A year later, with Myra's father, J.W., back in the fold as bass player and DIY manager/agent, Jerry Lee and company arrived in St. Louis, Missouri for a show, only to find that they'd trusted the wrong man, ex-manager Oscar Davis who'd promised, with Brown's personal cash, to rent the hall, blanket the city with promotion, and flood the radio with advertisements. They pulled into town to find no sponsorship or posters, and nothing on the radio. The result: a desultory, half-filled auditorium. Cornered, Davis said that St. Louis was a weird town anyway and promised that everything would be better in Kansas City. But Kansas City proved no more supportive of Jerry Lee than the Gateway City had been; there was, again, scant promotional backing for the show, which was poorly attended. Davis was fired, but a sad, decade-long routine was firmly in place: with his records nose-diving on the charts and his difficult and mercurial reputation increasing with his each no-show or tabloid entry, Jerry Lee Lewis could no longer be guaranteed packed houses. The hardcore fans who did show up were often vociferous in their adulation, but just as many casual fans hooted and jeered, called Jerry Lee a fag, and otherwise made their rancor and disdain palpable.

But the shows went on — he needed the money. "We worked small nightclubs and knockdown, drag-out joints and everything else," buddy and road manager Cecil Harrelson remembered. "We worked, built a circuit up, and we got to where we was working fifteen to twenty days a month, and then we got up to twenty to twenty-five days a month, and we would make the circuit, pack these nightclubs, no record label backing us up at all. Man, we was strictly doing it on our own. I remember the first seven or eight years I worked for Jerry. Hell, I don't think I heard ten of his songs on the radio. That's just how bad it was."

A look at the records released, and other tracks cut at Sun, between Ground Zero of the Setback in 1958 and Jerry Lee's last for Sun Records in 1963 reveals a fascinating barometer not only of his artistic choices — some smart, some misguided — but of the state of commercial rock & roll in the years leading up to the worldwide arrival of the Beatles. Buddy Holly, the Big Bopper, and Ritchie Valens had died in the epochal plane crash on February 3, 1959, Elvis was in the Army until 1960, maintaining a tenuous hold on the radio while gearing himself up for Hollywood, Chuck Berry was facing legal woes under the Mann Act, Eddie Cochran was killed and Gene Vincent seriously injured in seperate automobile crashes in England in 1960, Johnny Cash, Roy Orbison, and Carl Perkins had left Sun for varying success on major record labels — rock & roll was in an odd, unexpected, and somewhat crippling phase. And there was Jerry Lee Lewis in Memphis, toiling at 706 Union (later, 639 Madison Avenue), issuing single after disappearing single and cutting hundreds of tracks, searching for that elusive marriage of his singular style and the wallets of Americans.

The second 45 released after the English tour was conceived before Jerry Lee had left the States. Charlie Rich, a young songwriter and performer years away from his own stardom, had been awarded both sides of the new record, which he and Sun had hoped — expected? — would wrestle with "High School Confidential," released just prior to the U.K. tour, in Jerry Lee's assault on the American charts. But of course "Break Up," backed with "I'll Make It All Up To You," was maneuvering tentative footholds on a *Billboard* chart dotted with cultural landmines, and it peaked on the Pop charts at #52. Not a disgraceful showing, but hardly what Jerry Lee and Sun wanted, especially compared with what they'd already enjoyed: "Whole Lotta Shakin' Goin' On" (#3); "Great Balls Of Fire" (#2); "Breathless" (#7); "High School Confidential" (#21). Magic numbers, dreams made tangible.

Nothing much needs to be added to what's been written about the enchantment, joy, and innovation of those first singles, about the physicality, joy, and propulsion of them, or about their history. It's fascinating to listen to the sides cut by Jerry Lee *after* the scandal, especially the tracks recorded nearest in time to these myth-making first singles. Days, weeks, months, years — calendars are man-made toe-holds on a random, chaotic universe: "Break Up" was recorded three brief months after "High School Confidential," but a continent of sorry events occurred in between to make those 90-some days feel like a decade. But, given that "Break Up" had been demoed before the U.K. tour — by Jerry Lee, solo at his piano, likely days before the tour began — we can slot it aesthetically and spiritually with the Killer's classic singles. How does it stand up?

"Break Up" is a good rock & roll song, not a great rock & roll song. Missing? The mystery and mood, the Sun Studio air of Southern magic and timelessness, the resonance of strings and skin and analog waves. Robert Palmer describes an aspect of the Memphis pop accident well, the simpatico between Jerry Lee and his drummer, Jimmy Van Eaton. Citing the city of New Orleans (Little

Richard's drummer Earl Palmer, in particular) as the origin point for the kinds of rhythms percolating and filtered at Sun Studio, Palmer writes that the Big Easy "was the only municipality in the United States where African slaves were allowed to make and play drums after the early eighteenth century, and you could still hear African drumming in the city's Congo Square on the eve of the Civil War. The Black barrelhouse pianists of Louisiana and Mississippi, the ones who shaped Jerry Lee Lewis' music, were one-man African drum orchestras, weaving complex cross-rhythms between their left and right hands while maintaining a driving momentum." Lewis and Van Eaton were, Palmer adds, "inheritors of the same tradition, which partially explains their phenomenal rapport."

Jim Dickinson, longtime Memphis musician and producer who played piano and sang on the Jesters' rollicking "Cadillac Man," one of the final Sun singles, explains further: "Rock & roll is about the eighth notes and how you handle eight-over-four, the way the shuffle is felt. On the Sun records, Jimmy Van Eaton is utterly brilliant, and brings almost as much to the table as Jerry Lee does. He's playing a full-on shuffle but you can't hear it because there's no mike on the hi-hat. But everyone in the room, including Jerry Lee, could hear it and feel it." Phillips' lo-fi recording process captured and channeled the spirit bursting forth from Jerry Lee's waist-high spinet piano. "A lot of it had to do with the fact that it had two sources on the session floor," Dickinson continues. "There was a mike on the piano, of course, and there was Jerry Lee's vocal mike, an RCA Victor mike that was open all the way around. So there's twice as much piano! Phillips had the mike behind the piano, and the piano pushed up against the wall for separation. That was a primitive thing, but it trapped the sound. And Jerry Lee played so hard that there was just an attack, an inexplicable attack in what he did."

When he was pressed, Jerry Lee would later famously insist (though the answer sometimes felt like shtick) that his chief influences were Al Jolson, Jimmie Rodgers, and Hank Williams — occasionally he'd add Moon Mullican — three infamous *stylists* and larger-than-life personalities who cut intense, mythic, popular figures, and who were idolized, rightly so, as trail-blazers. But there were also Gospel and Black influences at work on Jerry Lee: the twin pulls of Ferriday's Assembly of God Church and Haney's Big House, light and dark, ascended and damned. What Sun Studio was able to do, with remarkable consistency and nerve in the mid- and late 1950s, was recognize, synthesize, and celebrate these sources. The stunning result was music — played by white folk coming out of tiny radios — that lifted off the tops of listeners' heads. "I still remember as a young kid vividly seeing Jerry Lee on television for the first time on *Dance Party*, a local live TV dance show in Memphis," Dickinson says. "He was playing as a trio, and his first record was about to come out. Some of my friends from East High School were on the show that day, dancing. And when he started playing, they literally laughed at him, because he was playing piano. But by the time he was through they weren't laughing anymore. "I was sitting in front of the TV crying like a baby. Here was a white man playing rock & roll on the piano. The images and the sound came together for the first time."

Such magic is largely absent in "Break Up" and, it must be said, in many of the singles released by Jerry Lee over the next six years. Van Eaton and guitarist Billy Riley synch-up nicely in a swaying rhythm, Jerry Lee grins his way appealingly through the vocal, one can picture the poodle skirts flying around the dance floor, but the record sounds a bit tentative after the colossal self-assurance of his first singles. Perhaps such a pull-back was inevitable — how long could the Killer make records like "Great Balls Of Fire" (the recording of which was prefaced by an infamous on-mike argument between Jerry Lee and Sam Phillips about the sinning ways made manifest in the song) before he combusted on his bench and took down the whole studio with him? If the records he released after the scandal betray a soreness and concern with coddling the market and industry in the correct ways, they also reflect, perhaps, a native scaling back of Jerry Lee's intensity.

His next single, "I'll Sail My Ship Alone" backed with "It Hurts Me So," was recorded and released in November of 1958. Jerry Lee sounds looser, more comfortable here — he sounds like he's having more fun on the Moon Mullican a-side, perhaps believing that the radio blackout and era of one-off shows in small venues was fated to end real soon. The absurdly apt title of the a-side would beg otherwise: commercially and culturally, Jerry Lee Lewis was to become an isolated and increasingly polarizing figure. "I'll Sail My Ship Alone" dropped off the *Billboard* Pop Singles chart after one pathetic week, and then disappeared for good.

Jerry Lee made greater music at Sun than what was officially released. Frustratingly, for Jerry Lee and his fellow musicians, much of it remained in the cans, deemed unworthy and un-commercial or otherwise plain wrong by Phillips and company, until liberated via legal and licensing avenues later in the 1960s and into the 1970s and 1980s. Some of the music is among Jerry Lee's best: "That Lucky Old Sun," a moving song recorded solo at the piano in late 1956 or early 1957, is one of Jerry Lee's most affecting vocals — his oft-cited spiritual stirrings feeling lived-in here — until his hardcore country readings later in the 1960s and 1970s surveyed the wreckage of his life in deeper ways; "Sixty Minute Man," "Keep Your Hands Off It/Birthday Cake," and "Cool, Cool Ways" are filthy fun, the kind of lubricious, lip-smacking odes that parents rightly found alarming; "Real Wild Child" (later covered and made popular by Iggy Pop) might've been a scorching single had it been released, but the title betrays the dilemma faced by controversy-shy Sun; "Sick and Tired" was raw, primal rock & roll; and a sultry version of "Be-Bop-a-Lula," among his last recordings for Sun in 1962, is an overlooked gem, a full-band honky-tonk tussle with Gene Vincent's trademark number that transforms it finally, and unsurprisingly, into the Killer's.

As Phillips and so many others have pointed out over the years, Jerry Lee's greatest gift was his innate ability to make any song his own, to galvanize a listener within the opening moments into intuiting *this can only be Jerry Lee Lewis* — even before The Killer hollers his own name. But he had to work at it — such personal investment in song didn't always come so easy. What seems to have crippled Jerry Lee in the years leading up to his departure from Sun was a self-conscious approach to songmaking, urged on him by Phillips, the market, commercial pressures from nearby Nashville, and ultimately by newer and newer waves of pop music and rock & roll. His 1961 version of the Motown classic "Money" is a prime example: squealing horns and faux-gospel backing vocals from the Anita Kerr Singers all but bury Jerry Lee under his own song, damping the considerable heat of his personality. The freshness and spontaneity of so many of the early sessions were necessarily sacrificed by practical concerns and marketplace insecurities.

But he would still occasionally drop a hot single. The February 1959 offering was the rollicking "Lovin' Up A Storm" backed with "Big Blon' Baby." Both tracks are vintage Killer, especially the flip, an under-two-minute ode to the titular woman featuring a smirking bounce in the beat and stop-start vocals echoing the lasciviousness of "Breathless." The record was critically well-received — both *Billboard* and *Cashbox* heralded its arrival in gusty commercial optimism — but again it tanked on the charts, bottoming out at #81 on the Top 100. A 1962 b-side, "Ramblin' Rose" (scorched to earth seven years later by the MC5 on their seminal live album *Kick Out The Jams*), was also great. Recorded during the sessions that produced the comparatively stiff "Money," muscled by the same large backing band including seven(!) horn players and an organist, the filthy standard slinks along in Jerry Lee's sure command, a sexy groove made all the more effective by its natural vibe. He got under the skin of this one.

Meanwhile, his commercial and personal woes continued, leavened by the occasional bright spot. In December of 1961 Sun issued his second album, *Jerry Lee's Greatest*, compiled of recent singles and studio tracks. In the spring of 1960 he'd embarked on a second tour of Australia and another week in Hawaii, playing to large and appreciative crowds, and there were several more appearances on television with Alan Freed and on Dick Clark's *American Bandstand*. He followed the latter show with a raucous appearance in Atlantic City in front of thousands at the Steel Pier. Jerry Lee wasn't commanding $10,000 paydays anymore, but he was playing in front of larger crowds and was beginning to enjoy longer engagements — including a successful run in Las Vegas — beyond the one-night-stands that he'd been enduring since 1958.

In 1960, he gathered with Van Eaton, Roland Janes, and other musicians for a recording session in Sam Phillips' new state-of-the-art studio at 639 Madison in Memphis, a few blocks from Union. A consequence of the label's success, Phillips had made the move as he'd felt confined in the cramped, corner studio and longed for bigger, more elaborate digs that would give him, his staff, and the musicians more room to play and relax. As John Floyd notes in *Sun Records: An Oral History*, the old control room was simply too small to house the newer, more sophisticated equipment that Sun, still a small outfit despite its recent triumphs, needed in order to stay competitive in the new decade. What Phillips unveiled was a "lavishly appointed" facility with a recording studio "about twice the size of the original studio, offices for everyone (plus a wet bar and jukebox in the boss' quarters), and live echo chambers that — in theory, at least, rendered obsolete Phillips' reliable but archaic slapback tape method." Archaic but eternal. The photos of Phillips smiling and posing proudly in his new studio show a man gamely embracing the space age of recording technology; at the cusp of the 1960s Phillips must've felt the pressure to compete in a larger, technologically modern arena. Gone forever were the homespun simplicity of 706 Union and the magic created there.

Jerry Lee would split his recordings between the new Sun studio and Phillips Studio in Nashville. Among the tunes cut at the latter facility was Ray Charles' "What'd I Say?" Jerry Lee felt cool and comfortable from the moment he tried out the opening notes, and the fellas in the studio felt something special about this one. Jimmy

Gutterman notes that at the end of the take Sam Phillips cheered. Against the notion that he would disappear beneath the bed of sessions players and overdubs, "this time Jerry Lee was completely uninhibited," Gutterman says, "so much that even the overdubbed backing singers (brought in to remind listeners of Charles' Raelettes, who had accompanied the original hit) did not detract from his raving, shouting, and pleading. The only thing wrong with it was that it ended too soon." Not too soon for the record-buying public, who put "What'd I Say" on the radio; it reached the highest position on the pop singles chart (#30) that Jerry Lee had seen in years and fared even better on the more hospitable black (#26) and country (#27) singles charts. This in turn lifted the perceived blacklist even more. Now that the alarm and uproar against his marriage to Myra had dissipated somewhat, and he was proving a larger and still exciting draw on the road — on Labor Day in 1961 he headlined a show for Murray "The K" at the Paramount Theatre in Brooklyn, New York — he was itching to capitalize, to move forward, to again become the center of attention.

But mired in a Sun contract that wouldn't expire until 1963, he had few options. As Gutterman observes, in the early 1960s Jerry Lee, while weathering the fickle trends in popular major-label pop music, had become an unwitting victim of "one of the aspects of Sun Records that made it great: its devotion to new talent, the flip side of which was a reliance on such performers." He adds, "Sun was not constructed like a major label that could nurture long-term careers. Until Motown changed the rules in 1963, regional independent labels thrived on novelty, not familiarity. The major labels treated Sun like a Triple-A baseball team; it was built for people to develop and move on to the big time." As Jerry Lee watched Elvis and Cash and Orbison decamp for the fertile and well-moneyed fields of the large, coastal labels — staffed with publicists and promoters who religiously sent out advance copies of singles and albums to radio stations, and with advertising departments willing to spend big and to spend nation-ally — he was caught at Sun, rereading common musical themes and styles in futile stabs at recapturing commercial triumphs.

"Any disgruntled observer could have seen that Jerry Lee had outgrown Sun," Gutterman says plainly.

So he continued to hit the road, reminding, testifying, essaying the strength of the piano by his mighty hands and the few overzealous fans leaping on top. Remarkably, given the staying power of the marriage scandal as the major trope in the narrative of Jerry Lee's career, he returned to England for a successful tour in 1962. The event was dark-ened, however, by an unconscionable tragedy for Jerry Lee and Myra when their young son Steve drowned in the family swimming pool on Easter Sunday. This was the first in a series of familial calamities suffered over the years by Jerry Lee, whose abuse of alcohol and drugs began to muscle its way unhappily and enduringly into his personal and professional life. But the U.K. tour was booked well in advance and Jerry Lee was contracted to play. Grieving, he, friend and road manager Cecil Harrelson, drummer Ernie Bowman, and Sun Records' Jud Phillips flew over in late April, and on the 29th began a bleary but hugely successful three-week run in the very country that four years prior had denounced him.

After the tour, Jerry Lee penned a grateful and gracious farewell to England that ran in *Disc* magazine. "When I stepped off that plane three weeks ago I didn't know what was happening to me," he wrote. "I didn't know whether the fans were going to accept me or whether I was going to be sent packing again. One of the greatest thrills of my performing career was that first night at Newcastle. I didn't know whether I would die the proverbial death or be carried shoulder high outside. . . . I have really worked hard at every stop. My, how those fans take it out of you! I have been kicked, pushed and kissed around every stage I have stood on. It is difficult to recall what has happened to me in the past few weeks in Britain as everything has gone at such a terrific pace — have you ever tried to count the telegraph poles that rip past you on a train? That is how I feel." He would return to England within the year, adding Germany and France to the itinerary, and these visits would prove not only lucrative but crucial toward reestablishing Jerry Lee Lewis as an undeniably powerful presence and as a loose-limbed, boastful spokesman for American rock & roll.

A German newspaper account of a May, 1963 show at the Star-Club in Hamburg describes fans packing the club and witnessing a riotous, sweaty show. Afterward, the reporter described a spent Jerry Lee backstage: "The last notes of the last song, his 'What'd I Say,' faded away and a wave of applause crashed over him. He graciously, and with his last strength, accepted the jubilation of his fans, until finally, his manager escorted him backstage. Jerry was completely pale. He asked for a tranquilizer, some cold water, and he stripped naked. Now dressed in a bathrobe, he toppled over. A doctor was quickly summoned, and he diagnosed a simple dizzy spell. It was nothing serious, but still!" Lest Jerry Lee's wild-man reputation be threatened, the writer hastened to add, "In two days Jerry could already continue traveling on his guest appearance tour, which featured many capital cities in Europe."

Praise was effusive. Of a Town Hall performance in Birmingham, England on May 6, Alan Stinton in the *Record Mirror* wrote, "No matter what you have read, no matter what you have heard, watching Jerry Lee Lewis on stage always produces a profound shock for the ears, the eyes and the very soul.... What Jerry does on stage is so beyond the realms of human imagination that no one can fully anticipate the aura of sheer excitement which he creates." British band the Outlaws (notable as eccentric producer Joe Meek's house band on many recordings) backed Jerry Lee on this 1963 tour. Guitarist Ken Lundgren recalls some political necessities of the era: "The Berlin corridor was still in effect and we had to travel with special permission, playing American bases with transport provided by the U.S. military," he says. One essential requirement of playing with the Killer transcended all geo-political concerns. "Jerry Lee was great to work with as long as you could hold the beat. That was his main thing." As Lundgren recalls, the Outlaws were likely "the most American-style rhythm section recording in Britain at the time," so, thankfully, Jerry Lee enjoyed their accompaniment, not to mention their considerable road shenanigans.

"That '63 tour was a memory," says Chas Hodges, who played bass in the Outlaws. "I floated through it on a cloud of Rock & Roll heaven. One day in Berlin we did *six* gigs. All at different venues." Hodges, too, recalls Jerry Lee's considerable Ferriday *say-so*. "Our drummer at the time said he would hate to back Jerry Lee because you don't know what he's going to do next. I said that was exactly why I love backing him." He adds, "I saw him worse for wear only once on that tour, and then only slightly. It was

at of the end of the six-gig stint in Berlin. He didn't toler-
ate bad or 'slow on the uptake' musicians. I wasn't one of
them so we got on like a house on fire."

For the Killer, the '62 and '63 tours were more good
tutoring in how to plug yourself in to what matters in the
face of ridicule or — worse? — indifference.

Jerry Lee's final singles for Sun trickled out in 1962 and
1963, none of them particularly interesting. He was
riding out his contract and his sights were fixed higher.
Between the release of his final two singles for Sam Phillips
("Teenage Letter" and "Carry Me Back To Old Virginia")
he found and inked a new manager. Frank Casone was
a Memphis-based hotel and private-club owner with an
Italiano swagger and rough edge that appealed to Jerry
Lee. He'd secured the singer the Las Vegas engagement
for an eye-popping $10,000 a week, Jerry Lee's juiciest
payday in five years.

Casone's chief interest was in negotiating a new record
deal for Jerry Lee. He talked cigars and percentages with
Columbia, RCA, Mercury, and Liberty Records — all the
while fielding renewal offers from Phillips, who knew
that he'd have trouble with the competing bids and was
thus eager to include a clause, protecting his discovery, in
any deals that Jerry Lee might sign. In essence, Phillips
wanted the right to continue to release Jerry Lee's Sun-
recorded tracks for the foreseeable future. "He held me
to that contract with Sun for five long years," Jerry Lee
complains in his autobiography, "knowing all the time he
had no distributors for my records. Why he done that I
don't understand, but he did."

Phillips was keen to hold on to Jerry Lee's name for
personal as well as professional reasons — he strongly felt

the sting of abandonment as one by one his artists left Sun for higher profiles. "Because it's a child-bearing kind of situation," he explained. "You feel you've given unselfishly and you've gambled on them from the front end with your talent, your time, with your energies. When they left me, I didn't blame them personally, because I knew the stories they had heard. And the stories were simple — no matter if I had been giving them ten percent — 'Man, is that all you're getting?' These people were unsuspecting. It was their first contract. Their first adventure into the world of business and a little money. When they get a damned check for $50,000 — can you imagine? They hadn't seen that much money in their lifetime or in their daddy's lifetime."

After ironing out details with Phillips over distribution and royalty payments, Casone settled with Mercury Records, a Chicago-based label that, in addition to signing Jerry Lee to that fabled $50,000 contract, guaranteed him a two-album-per-year deal and robust national promotion. This fighter's stratagem appealed to Jerry Lee, who'd been smarting from what he perceived as Phillips' lethargy. "Phillips promised that Jerry would see a third album on Sun Records, and even announced the fact to the press," music historian Colin Escott notes. "However, it failed to materialize. The pop marketplace was firmly in the grip of the album age by 1963. Singles still outsold albums on a raw count but the margins were so much better on albums and returns were lower. It was in everyone's interest to produce albums." Phillips, meanwhile, "still saw Lewis as a singles artist. Perhaps the sales figures on the two Jerry Lee Lewis Sun albums were the foundation of this belief." At Mercury, Jerry Lee would work with producers Shelby Singleton and Jerry Kennedy and release singles and albums on the newly minted Smash affiliate label. He signed on September 20, 1963, days after his last single for Sun had been released to a characteristically yawning *Billboard* charts. Jerry Lee and Myra celebrated the new deal along with the birth of their second child, daughter Phoebe, born on August 30.

Hot to record, eyeing an upcoming $5,000 per week residency at the Chez Paree club in Chicago in October, Jerry Lee felt rejuvenated and worthwhile. Two days after signing, he and a team of accomplished session musicians holed up in Phillips Studio in Nashville with Singleton, whose opening salvo was to have the Killer re-record his best-known songs. An ill-fated, cautionary step in the singer's comeback, this allowed the producer and label to gauge the current commercial interest in Jerry Lee against prevailing music trends, and to buy some time to solicit new original material to record. Jerry Lee shrugged his shoulders, liquored-away any suspicion or skepticism he might've felt, and burned through two sessions revisiting the enigmas and thrills in the songs conceived at Sun.

The results were anemic and odd, even four decades down the line. The opening 25 seconds of "Whole Lotta Shakin' Goin' On," the first number tackled by Jerry Lee at the sessions, reveal the nature of the problem: so crude and essential as recorded by Jack Clement in 1957, the song is garlanded in Nashville with crisply-EQ'ed hi-hat percussion, an intrusive walking electric bass, and a syncopated rhythm guitar that feels like an annoying kid brother tagging along looking for some hijinks. The reverb applied to Jerry Lee's voice sounds contrived and artificial after Phillip's hands-on magic-making at 706 Union, and sweetened with chirpy female backing singers who were meant to complement but end up sounding as if they'd wandered into the wrong party. Sighs Escott, "'Whole Lotta Shakin' Goin' On' needed a chorus like it needed a polka band joining Jerry on the break."

"High School Confidential" fared a bit better — the singers and horn/rhythm guitar arrangement felt clumsily attached, as if Jerry Lee was someone's weird uncle with whom the junior high kids were forced to play, but the song's driving force is still there, as is Jerry Lee's sure, double-time, right-hand galloping and left-hand riffing. Throughout the sessions he played well and gamely, but too often his persona — here both traded-on *and* forged, an awkward tug-and-pull if there ever was one — sighs and gives in to the slick studio proceedings. "Your Cheatin' Heart" was an interesting attempt; Jerry Lee had recorded an unreleased version of the Hank Williams classic for Phillips three years earlier and here he sings the song with so much respect that it nearly transcends the junior-high auditorium vibe. But "Great Balls of Fire" shouldn't have been attempted. A purist's complaint? Maybe, but his greatest recorded moments at Sun were like the weather, they filled every inch of the room as only atmosphere can, and how can you replicate that? "Frustrating," lamented Jerry Kennedy, a guitarist at these sessions and Jerry Lee's future producer. "We missed the feel. We couldn't recapture the feel of those early hits."

The winkingly-titled *The Golden Rock Hits Of Jerry Lee Lewis* was released on Smash Records on January 1, 1964. The evening before, an optimistic Jerry Lee played at the Mercury-Smash label convention in downtown Chicago, gamely helping tipsy executives and secretaries twist in the New Year. Mercury marketed the release in an avalanche of promotion. In the overreaching liner notes — the word "dynamic" is breathlessly employed twice in the first two paragraphs — Eddie Kilroy gushed that the album "scores the polish and finesse Jerry Lee has acquired since his career first bolted into view. . . . Excitement and fire he still has . . . but there's a finer and even more thrilling 'something new' that spotlights him as a greater artist with a lifetime of recordings in the future." Optimistic if vaguely defensive stuff.

New or otherwise, *The Golden Rock Hits Of Jerry Lee Lewis* sold respectably, though disappointingly. "In commercial terms though, it was the right horse for the course," Escott insists. "The album broke into the pop charts and seemed to vindicate Singleton's faith in signing Lewis." But the enduring fact that Shelby Singleton couldn't escape was embodied in his very surname: "It was hit singles that really sparked action in the album market," Escott declares. "Now that all the old hits were on an album, Jerry needed new hits and therein lay the problem."

Roughly a decade later — at the end of a long, uneasy journey through licensing offices, marketing meetings, and cut-throat strategy sessions — the version of "Breathless" cut at these sessions was pressed onto *20 Rockin' Originals*, packed into cardboard boxes and onto freight trucks, driven along highways, and stocked into a nondescript chain department store in suburban Washington, D.C. where my parents purchased a copy. In the rec room, I listened to this version of "Breathless" and knew that something was off, was wrong. Something felt queer, Jerry Lee sounded hollow, nearly artificial, erstwhile. ("Frustrating. We missed the feel. We couldn't recapture the feel . . .") Watching the Pickwick label revolve on the turntable, goofing on the mock-1950s vibe of the cover even as I fell for it, secretly lusting for the model on the front, I listened to "Breathless" trying to work its way through me but hemmed in by its own contrivances, and Jerry Lee Lewis sounded lost.

FOUND

People get so high on the myth of Jerry Lee that often many forget that the guy sings and plays piano.

—Jimmy Gutterman

April 5, 1964, a sunny Sunday morning. About a hundred teenage boys and girls gather at the relative calm of Marylebone Train Station in central London. On cue from Richard Lester, the kids begin shrieking and running frantically *en masse* down Boston Place, chasing John Lennon, George Harrison, and Ringo Starr. The three young men miraculously manage to dodge the flock of fans and duck into the station where there to greet them are Paul McCartney (in disguise), more euphoric, piercing teenage screams, and cultural lunacy.

This is the opening sequence of *A Hard Day's Night*, of course, the movie that dramatizes Beatlemania in all its glory, machinations, and ecstasy. The title track and the scenes of the herd of fans nearly trampling Harrison — he'd fallen while running for his life while Lennon laughs uproariously, still chugging for his own safety — are among the most memorable openings of any modern film, and the subsequent 90 minutes went a long way toward solidifying the Beatles' permanent place in popular culture. It was a stunning force of talent, luck, and promotion: a few months before filming of the movie began, the Beatles had performed before millions on *The Ed Sullivan Show* and, the day before lensing, learned to their collective disbelief that they'd secured the top five positions on the American *Billboard* Hot 100, an unheard-of domination of teenagers' ears, hearts, and wallets. Left behind was a vacuum in which many musicians, some wildly popular before 1964, found themselves grasping for relevance.

On that same April 5th, Jerry Lee Lewis arrived in Hamburg, West Germany. He was scheduled to play that evening at the Star-Club, a newish venue on the sordid Reeperbahn made internationally famous by that same group of Liverpudlians who'd go a long way toward stealing the Killer's considerable sex-and-gospel fervor. The Beatles had last played the Star-Club in 1962 but their worldwide ascendance two years later would forever brand the raucous venue as "that German place where the Beatles played."

The region has long breathed an independent, distinctive air, piquant with sea salt and cut through with cool. It is named for the Hammaburg Castle built by Emperor Charlemagne in 808 AD; periods of ebbing waves of prosperity and discord followed as the country suffered Viking invasions and short-lived annexation by Napoleon. One of the world's great and historic sea ports was blessed with its proximity on the River Elbe, a 680-mile-long, quarter-mile-wide waterway that engraves northwestern Germany from its North Sea origin. Centuries ago, the harbor city belonged to the Hanseatic League, a medieval alliance of trading guilds that dominated northern European trade and amassed considerable commercial might. Although the League was eventually dissolved and the participating cities brought under national rule, the city was allowed to keep a certain autonomous status that it celebrates to this day with cultural flair. As journalist William Triplett has noted, "an aristocratically hip atmosphere predominates in the Free and Hanseatic City of Hamburg, Germany."

The metropolis has a dynamic history of both strife and renewal. A huge fire in May of 1842 destroyed a quarter of the city, and historian Martin Middlebrook describes the massive, large-hearted, four-decade reconstruction as nothing less than the birth of modern Hamburg. The rebuilding allowed the city to thrive well into the twentieth century as a cultural, well-heeled urban capital renowned for its architecture, massive churches with copper-plated spires, towers and masts, and museums. The Weimar Republic and Adolph Hitler nearly destroyed a country that by the mid-1940s had become choked and decimated by economic depression, the bitterly costly European war, and the Allied bombings. Only the bravery and foresight of one Gauleiter Kaufmann, a Nazi party ruler who defied Hitler's waning-days edict to defend Hamburg at any cost against the Allies, spared the city an even grimmer future when Hamburg surrendered to the Allies in the Spring of 1945. Mercifully relieved of bombing and street brawls, the city began its long and painful post-war reconstruction, aided in part by its politically decreed and providential location in the free West — not communist East — Germany. As Hamburg crawled from the literal and figurative rubble of the War, the city continued to benefit from the timeless Elbe and its traffic in commerce, and from the city rulers' progressive attitudes.

Alan Clayson in *Hamburg: The Cradle of British Rock* quotes the city's chief of police, writing dazedly after the blitzkrieg: "The marks left on the face of the town can never be erased ... hazy impressions of a blackened city of Wagnerian apocalypse with parking lots formed from bomb sites were as undone as any of a flickering, monochrome Hamburg with horse-drawn carriages in a silent movie." Those arriving in Hamburg after the war were surprised, discovering "a modern metropolis recovered more fully than equally shell-shocked Coventry, Dover, Newcastle and the like would be for years, thanks to more forceful urban renewal programme, both helped and hindered by the attentions of the [Royal Air Force]." Middlebrook relates that much of Hamburg, in the form of sturdily constructed bomb shelters, eyesore embarrassments to so many, and mass War-era cemeteries, offered its citizens visceral, physical reminders of the mid-century discord but that, gradually, these unhappy urban *Anzeigen* were complemented by the growth of capital regeneration, civic pride, and a kind of national tolerance of a miserable but undeniable history. The Hamburg port presently thrives — annually some 11,000 ships drop anchor there for business — and the city has long turned its attention from the darkened past to a more colorful sense of that past: the 2,496 bridges, more than any other city in the world, the flourishing arts scenes and museums, and the crowing fact that Hamburg is home to more millionaires than any other German city.

It's often said that Hamburg is unlike much of the rest of Germany. "With the city's long history of independence, the inhabitants of Hamburg had developed a character all of their own," Middlebrook observes, from its English-style architecture along the Elbe and rich personal history with Britain, to the matchless manner of its citizens in their liberal acceptance of diverse and often iconoclastic lifestyles. Travel writer Denny Lee notes the city's "jarring juxtapositions"; the waterfront "heaves with rusty docks, while its center is filled with emerald parks, blue lakes and cream-colored villas. ... Despite playing second fiddle to the cultural juggernaut that is Berlin, Hamburg breeds its own brand of the cosmopolitan cool — with a large Turkish population, gay enclaves and fashion centers — who mingle at chichi restaurants and steamy underground clubs."

A particularly stark and lively contrast emerges when one realizes that the city's old-money enclaves sit so near Hamburg's most notorious area, the St. Pauli district and its infamous Reeperbahn. Known in German as *die sündige*

Meile — "the sinful mile" — the four-lane, quarter-mile-long street along the north banks of the Elbe has long been home to a permissive red-light district (Germany's oldest region for the world's oldest profession), teeming with all-night sex shops, strip clubs, smut theatres, bars, and nightclubs. Sex is the power that endures, and the Reeperbahn perpetually hums.

It's wildly appropriate that Jerry Lee Lewis' greatest rock & roll album would be made on the Reeperbahn, and that it would be made at this particular troubled point in the Killer's career, as the infamous street grew from a haven for the outcast and the shamed. The St. Pauli district originated in the seventeenth century as a small suburb lurking outside the gates of Hamburg, built there for defense purposes and eventually deemed less crucial as various tensions eased; in due course, any business or practice considered unfit for the city proper, such as warehouses or plague hospitals, were suitably banished to the other side of the gates. Thus emerged a home for the unwelcome. Throughout the eighteenth century, roving sailors spilling into Hamburg from docked ships were asked to move their libidinous behavior from the more respectable areas north of the river down to the Reeperbahn, which soon became the refuge for a newly liberated seaman to find a comely prostitute or two with whom to spend a glorious, lager-fueled, bed-rocking evening.

A union-bedeviled misfit like Jerry Lee would've likely enjoyed the fact that, as Gunter Zint relates to Spencer Leigh in *Twist and Shout: Merseybeat, The Cavern, The Star-Club, and the Beatles*, "if you had a profession and you were not union, you could go to [St. Pauli] and work as a shoemaker . . . It was just outside Hamburg, so everything that was new or funny or anti-establishment was there." A century or so earlier, Catholic nuns who had found themselves unaccepted by the authorities of the local Protestant orders were unceremoniously urged to move their worshipping south to the more seamy, if still convivial, St. Pauli district, which became over time a zone of incongruous churches. By the mid-twentieth century, visiting musicians "stuck between the sensuality of their new surroundings and their own ingrained compliance to Christian values," Leigh writes, "would take sheepish communion at the Roman Catholic church next door to the Star-Club." Jerry Lee would've gotten off and been chastened by the resulting tension: "When such a person looked about the pews, a wave of shame would swamp him when he recognized a *bar-frau* whose breasts, now swaddled decently, he had squeezed the night before." From welcoming horny sailors to tolerating religious freedom, such is the dual-contrast that has long ruled the Reeperbahn, where the sun rises and sets on 24-hour sex shops and 24-hour churches. Jerry Lee would record a live album on a side street named *Grosse Freiheit*, which in English translates literally as "large liberty." More colloquially it means "great freedom," the unofficial motto of the sinful mile.

Just the kind of sovereignty that Jerry Lee was looking for.

Among the tracks cut at the September, 1963 Nashville sessions with Shelby Singleton and Jerry Kennedy was "Hit the Road, Jack," Ray Charles' #1 hit from two years earlier. Released on November 1, 1963, it was Jerry Lee's first single on Smash (if I write "smash single" I might better describe the soon-to-be-dashed hopes of Mercury executives). The performance was exciting and interesting:

liberated from exhuming his old hits, Jerry Lee bravely and sincerely sinks himself into Charles' kiss-off. Though still annoyingly crowded by a horn section, he sings above it, rising on the potency of his character, and his vocals mesh well with the back-up singers here, the kind of sass Charles heard in his head when he wrote the tune. The oddly-swinging, r&b-cum-honky-tonk arrangement works, and Jerry Lee's right-hand flourishes sound inborn, not superfluous. Most of all, Jerry Lee sounds like he really *likes* this number and is gonna have some fun with it. Anyone who was listening at the time might've held out some hope that the Killer was finding his way back to his own style again. As the primary salvo in Jerry Lee's new arsenal, the song was pretty auspicious — and failed miserably on the Pop charts, topping out at #100 before fading (the flip, "Pen and Paper," would fare considerably better on the always forbearing country charts, where it landed at the mid-#30s for a short while).

Buzzing from Mercury's and Casone's attention, Jerry Lee hit the long road again in the fall and winter of 1963/64, smirking at the still-low paydays, and enduring a string of one-night stands through the Midwest, but pleased and stoked by a week-long residency at the Thunderbird Lounge in Las Vegas. As *The Golden Rock Hits Of Jerry Lee Lewis* was being readied for release, Casone was busy arranging the details of another U.K. tour to include two shows in Germany, in Berlin and Hamburg. Buoyed by the responses of the English and Continental crowds a year earlier, Jerry Lee was amped to visit Europe again and was hopeful that — in addition to some good old-fashioned bourbon-and-lass *fun* — the tour might translate into healthier record sales.

Meanwhile, Mercury had gotten its corporate hands

on a song that everyone in the Windy City felt was going to be the hit that brought Jerry Lee back for good. The Angels had scored a mammoth #1 in 1963 with "My Boyfriend's Back," the kind of song that embodies the Brill Building ethos of pre-Beatles America: innocent but feisty; ultimately harmless, but muscled by urban energy and beehive-and-girdle sexuality. The song was written by the trio of Feldman/Goldstein/Gottehrer — Robert Feldman and Jerry Goldstein, who'd written the theme song to Alan Freed's *The Big Beat* television show, and Richard Gottehrer, a songwriter, and later a producer, who'd join them in 1960. The Manhattan trio had written a new song, "I'm On Fire," and were shopping it to producers and labels. It ended up in the batch of songs that Singleton and Jerry Lee were considering, and on February 14, 1964 at the RCA Victor Studio in Nashville, Jerry let it rip.

"'I'm On Fire' was the first time Jerry Lee's brand of elemental rock and roll made sense in this more orchestrated context," Jimmy Gutterman gushes, "referring to Sun triumphs without merely restating them. He had finally figured out how to make a big band rock." I beg to differ. History has been too kind to "I'm On Fire," the kind of self-conscious number inevitably associated with performers anxious to recapture a gloried past. Jerry Lee sings with as much zest as he could muster, but the stiff arrangement and cluttered rhythm section, not to mention the conscious and already dated "twist" beat, render the song quaint. (Feldman/Goldstein/Gottehrer would do much better in a year or two, dubbing themselves the Strangeloves and writing and scoring hits with "I Want Candy," "Cara-Lin," and "Night Time.")

Jerry Lee didn't need to revisit his past, he needed to

embrace what was mystifying about his best work: the conflict between lust and grace; the bone-simple, time-less arrangements of piano, guitars, drums; the happy accidents. On too many of Jerry Lee's 1960s recordings — before he would again embrace straightforwardness in the great country albums he'd make at the end of the decade — the horns and chirpy backing singers sound fussy, artificially layered, and, worse, like rude guests at a party who aren't nearly as funny as they think they are and who noisily push their way to the center of the room, competing with the host who doesn't have to try quite so hard.

But Jerry Lee had to try pretty hard in 1963 and 1964. And he was up against gale-strength winds. Big surprise: "I'm On Fire" took a swan dive on the pop charts, peak-ing at #98, sniffing the breezes coming across the pond from Big Beat England and running scared the other way. On the very day of the record's release, the Beatles were in London at EMI studios ripping through "Long Tall Sally" in a single take, laying waste to the foundation and then building upon the rubble of their r&b sources while whooping it up and grinning all the while. That these white kids from northern England could revise Little Richard the way Jerry Lee had revised, say, Otis Blackwell, and in as startling, fresh, and youthful a way as the Killer had done just a few years earlier . . . well, seismic changes were pushing everyone's needles into the red.

Jerry Lee and Smash were bitterly disappointed, and flabbergasted, at the continued stony commercial recep-tion toward the man who had helped create rock & roll less than a decade ago. Was a *sotto voce*, industry-wide obstruction of Jerry Lee still around? "It remains foggy whether the blacklist was a real one or just an excuse,"

Gutterman considers. "One Mercury executive of the time said eighteen years later, 'We had to blame it on something, didn't we? We couldn't say that *we* were the problem.'" Gutterman adds, "It is hard not to imagine that only a conspiracy could have kept off the radio performances this sturdy by a man with a history of million sellers."

With resolute if bloodshot eyes turned toward a blurry future, Jerry Lee hit the road again for a string of one-nighters in Florida. On March 18, 1964, a couple of weeks after "I'm On Fire" vanished from American radio for good, he and buddy Cecil Harrelson left Memphis, Tennessee for England. There, promoter Don Arden had arranged for an English group he'd signed to Decca Records, the Nashville Teens, to back Jerry Lee on a well-publicized, booked-solid, three-week tour. Jerry Lee arrived on March 19, one hand clutching a suitcase, the other his $11,500 guarantee.

He was about to make the best rock & roll of his vexed life.

He could've read the cracks in the goddamned ceiling, he was that close. The poor-man's throne was held aloft, and beneath it a crowd of hundreds craned their heads skyward in wonder, and what should rain down but great balls of fire.

Jerry Lee Lewis' performance on March 19, 1964 in *Whole Lotta Shakin' Goin' On*, broadcast on Granada television, is one of the great rock & roll TV programs of the era, and the first of a three-leg stomp across England and Germany where a bruised Jerry Lee would night after night show what a titan he still could be, performing, recording, and releasing some of the greatest music of his career. The Granada program was the first gig of the tour, and was born from Jerry Lee's live reputation. "I first met Jerry Lee Lewis at the concert at State Kilburn, and then the Bride Scandal blew up in the press here," recalls Johnnie Hamp, producer of the television show. "I was at that time booking one-night stands for the Granada group of theatres before I became a television producer, and I'd booked Lewis into Granada Tooting, which he had done before being banished." A few months before *Whole Lotta Shakin' Goin' On*, Hamp had produced a similar television show, *It's Little Richard*, through Don Arden. Richard had sweated out a typically fantastic and well-received performance, and Hamp wanted more. "I went to see Lewis at a club in Kingston, Surrey and booked him for the TV special."

Jerry Lee was driven by limousine from the airport directly to the television studio in Manchester. Gene Vincent was also on the bill, and the studio, buzzing with an intense, American Greaser Rockabilly vibe, was outfitted with a *Wild Ones*-cum-fashion-layout stage, designed by Michael Bailey after director Philip Casson's idea: hundreds of leather-clad, shades-wearing teenagers, lured in from nearby Manchester University, posing on a stacked, open-walled scaffolding alongside motorcycles. Casson recalls, "I had gotten in touch with the motorbike company and asked them if they'd be interested in delivering, and they actually did! The only thing I wanted to do and couldn't do was I wanted all of the horns put on the bikes to really rave it up a bit. But they wouldn't let me do that." Casson ordered that the crowd of bikes be driven along the Manchester streets and directly into the studio, roaring all the while, part of a combustible and eye-popping (and ear-ringing) pre-show.

Hamp had hired a fierce young band from northern

England, the Animals, as a warm-up act (they weren't televised but were so good that Hamp edited their performance into a video release of the show later) and by the time Vincent was finished with his rousing set the crowd was positively foaming. Battling jet-lag and calling on his storehouse of native energy, Jerry Lee strutted into the studio wearing a black suit, white shirt, dark tie, and pointy-toed white-leather shoes, and gave himself over to Hamp and Casson's masterstroke vision for his entrance: he would descend from the heavens unto the eager crowd courtesy of a hydraulic platform, on which a Challen grand piano, bench, and Fender amp had been ceremoniously and, Jerry Lee trusted, sturdily placed.

The crowd erupted when he hit the first chords of "Great Balls Of Fire," Jerry Lee sounding as if he characteristically expected his backing band — on this occasion the Flintstones — to know when he was going to kick it off, but they had to catch up from the start. Surveying his British kingdom, Jerry Lee grinningly works his way through the tune, held aloft a dozen feet in the air while the Flintstones bash away gleefully beneath him. His right leg pounding $4/4$, he whoops it up while couples clap and dance and twist and gape open-mouthed up at him. Casson's four-camera, multi-angle direction reflected the era's excitement with rock & roll's new rhythmic, sexually-playful, urban power. The cameras ("these big chunky things," Casson chuckles) moved with some difficulty among the dancing crowd, Casson nonetheless committed to capturing the reckless vibe of the floor. Rotary-lens shots move among aerial views of the dancing crowd and hip set design, medium shots of Jerry Lee at the piano, and close-ups of his already-perspiring (and, it must be said, somewhat puffy) face, where the cameras capture a telling mix of concentration, bemusement, and mild surprise. *I mean I know I'm this good and I know that I deserve it but really now* ... Jerry Lee loads up the song with his signature moves — the egocentric first-person references, the theatrically raised arms, the absurd glissandos, the pounding double-time right hand, the long blond hair threatening to bust loose from the pomade — so many moves, and so soon, that "Great Balls Of Fire," only seven years old, already sounds eternal, and the kids below him, flying around in their hyped-up jitterbug and swing moves, skirts flying, seem to feel that already. After the instrumental break, the stage begins to slowly descend. By the time Jerry Lee finishes the tune he's back on earth.

He slows things down a bit for "You Win Again." The leisurely-swinging changes of the Hank Williams tune allow the kids to dip in and out of the song's groove, and the Flintstones ease in naturally to this one (perhaps calmer now, and less cowed at playing a b-side than a hit). Jerry Lee caresses the loser ethos in the lyric, and Casson exploits the slower pace to indulge in abstract, extreme-close-ups of blurry hands, Jerry Lee's and the drummer's, edited with conventional medium-shots, translating the tension between arrangement and chaos, an intensity that Jerry Lee is already flirting with this early in the performance. "It was exactly what we wanted," Casson remembers of his and Hamp's work. "It was done with passion. Emotion, nothing clinical. Just the sweat and the blood."

At the end of the tune, Jerry Lee's itching to cut loose, and the last four songs of *Whole Lotta Shakin' Goin' On* make the performance legendary, as the wall between Jerry Lee and the audience, already on deliriously shaky foundations at this point in the program, comes crashing down. He wastes no time before launching into the filthy demands of "High School Confidential." As will happen a few weeks later on the Reeperbahn, the crowd erupts before Jerry Lee's finished his opening mandate. When he and the band come flying into the chorus 20 seconds later, something changes in the studio. Jerry Lee's shows were always a crash course in successful pacing — a six-song mini-concert no less so — and he smartly held off on this number until the crowd was well-oiled; Casson now cuts primarily to the dancing kids who are gradually crowding the piano which, though it was tied down with rope, begins to sway under the sweaty adulation. To the jaw-dropping notice of the audience watching later on television — many of whom might still have held the cradler-robber in great contempt — Jerry Lee plays the second half of the show amidst a sea of young, adoring bodies.

Two guys in particular, hanging out at the end of the piano, well within Jerry Lee's line of vision, look as if they're suffering — enjoying? — seizures, their heads bobbing maniacally and their fists clenched tight or flapping wildly against the joy of the detonating music. They're the emblematic duo for the mania, these two Manchester University laddies. Before Jerry Lee hits the solo, he's surrounded by dozens of kids clapping hands, yelling along, pounding their fists on the unfortunate piano. His hair beginning its wet, sexy bust-out, Jerry Lee lifts his right leg during the solo and pounds it on the keys to the shrieking delight of the crowd. "The only direction I gave to Jerry Lee was to do his own thing, jump on the piano if he felt it right," Hamp recalls. "The fans crowding round the piano was entirely spontaneous — we'd handpicked the audience insisting that they wear black leathers, shades, etc., to suit the motorbike and scaffold setting in the studio. They were all rock fans so it wasn't entirely unexpected, although it did restrict camera shots a bit." Hamp adds, in model English understatement, "The atmosphere made up for that." After a superfluous guitar solo — no one could really hear it beneath the yells and piano bashing — Jerry Lee brings the song crashing down and, in the rubble afterwards, the kids push even closer to the piano and thrust out their hands to congratulate this American maniac. "Thank you very much" Jerry Lee obliges, torn between keeping his profile to the camera (ever the pro) and glad-handing every kid who's pushing and pulling at his sleeves.

The delirium is in temporary abeyance. Lest anyone forget why Jerry Lee was in the U.K. he duly whips out "I'm On Fire" next ("a brand new one that was written and recorded . . . oh, about eighteen days ago," he announces) and, after pushing his hair back and responsibly informing all assembled that the record is out on the Philips label in England, lets loose the kind of performance that Singleton and Kennedy had hoped to capture back in Memphis: rockin', loose, fun, and funny. Head back, tongue lolling out obscenely during the double-time solos, Jerry Lee is getting nearer to everything scary and thrilling about him in this song — the girls with maracas and boys leaping about and hollering back only add to the craze. Able as they are, the backing band barely matters at this point; Casson has essentially stopped cutting to them, focusing instead on Jerry Lee and the audience, equally soaked in sweat at this point.

At the song's close, chuckling unabashedly now at the fervor of the hands thrust at him and slapping the piano top, he senses that the kids want the fast stuff to continue, want the myth-making numbers, but he has to do good by his hero Hank one more time and announces that he's gonna slow it down — "just a *little* bit!" he promises — for "Your Cheatin' Heart." Truth be told, the surrounding kids look a bit relieved to be able to catch their breath, and they swing and sway through the number. My favorite moment: one fella pauses long enough during Jerry Lee's flamboyant solo to lean over the piano, peer inside, and study the hammer-and-string guts in open-mouthed fascination.

"It was so instant. It was 'Hi Jerry, go man go!'" Casson marvels more than four decades later. "He was that kind of guy. All he wanted to do was get on the damn piano and do his stuff. And it was that kind of immediacy that we were aiming for. It wasn't controlled." He adds, "It's a dangerous thing to do, and you wouldn't be able to do it now. It was, *Go in and busk it and grab.*"

There's one song left for Jerry Lee to grab. Midway through a half-grinned "thankyouverymuch" he rumbles into "Whole Lotta Shakin' Goin' On," indulges in a lengthy intro, basking in the reception, and then frees his arsenal: before the second verse he dips his head and then throws it back wildly, unleashing his long hair in a spray of sweat; before the solo he stands and kicks the bench behind him off the riser; before the song is over he's a legend again. He plays the remainder of the song standing up, pounding his right hand on the keys when he's not facing the crowd, mike stand in hand, sayin' he ain't fakin'. In a priceless moment, the kid nearest, prep-cool in a dark jacket and chinos, reaches out and caresses Jerry Lee's golden locks for a moment as if they were dangling amulets, hoping to secure some follicle magic or maybe just to get off in an hysterical grab. For the next minute he stands wide-eyed and slack-jawed, inches away from the singer, once or twice daring to reach out and clasp him on the shoulder; next to him, his buddy leans on his shoulder and can't believe his great fortune. Jerry Lee shrugs and grins. *Shake, baby, shake.* Lay of the land. As the band plays behind him, looking for the cue for the song's finish, Jerry Lee lets loose one of the longest, most guttural, lascivious, and dirty *grrrrrrowls* of the show, puts the mike stand down, bends forward and, remarkably, lets his hair hang down — it's a foot long! — and runs his hands languorously through it like a teenage girl loving the warm sun at the public pool. I wonder if there wasn't some kind of unspoken flirting between Jerry Lee and the besotted kid near him, who tries in vain to reach out and touch Jerry Lee's hair as he's bent over. It's a sexy, dangerous, reckless, and comic moment.

It was also necessary *mach schau*, as Hamp recalls. "The only direction I gave to Jerry Lee was to end his set with 'Whole Lotta Shakin',"" he says. "But when he started the song it was obvious to me that it was too early, so I ran down to the studio floor and signaled to him to keep going until I gave him the wind up."

"Go!" Casson yelled at his crew. "We need more!"

So, forced to improvise, Jerry Lee used the hair-swinging and testifying to milk the crowd and to give him the room and the material to explore a bit. At this point, after yet another gallop through the chorus, he stands up from his crouched position and strips off his jacket, his soaked dress-shirt echoing the limp duck's-ass and greased-back hairdos collapsing in the heat all around him. He does an odd kind of shoulder-shake-shimmy and bellows at the crowd, now clearly in his element and loving it. He shakes his hair out again and drops back to his haunches, pounding the keys primitively, hollering at the crowd and exhorting them to push him even further, stands back up and brings his right foot up and crashing on the ivories — the kid next to him gropes a whole fistful of well-tailored cuff this time around — and, as the wild-eyed teens start pointing at the top of the piano, he stands up again, pulls the mike wire out of its tangle near the amp and, mike stand in hand, steps up on top of the piano to the glee of the crowd. He's back up in the air, now, surveying, pointing, gesturing, hair in his manic eyes, hoarsely commanding "Shake, baby, shake" as if the structure of the very building depended on it. By the end of the tune — all seven raucous minutes of it — Jerry Lee's wasted and exhausted, he can barely stand, a great shot from Casson showing the kids around the piano ogling the V of his crotch before the whole thing comes down. Given the signal from Casson, Jerry Lee finally winds it up, ending the tune standing atop the beaten, surrendered piano. The camera, with nowhere else to go, pans to the left revealing the program's credits emblazoned on a pair of motorcycles while the crowd hollers. Afterwards, worn out, Jerry Lee collapsed in the dressing room.

A week later he commented on the show in *Melody Maker*: "A real ball," he drawled.

While in England, Jerry Lee was asked by *New Musical Express* journalist Richard Green to hear some recent U.K. singles and to offer his comments, for a profile piece. The interesting article ran in the April 3 edition. Jerry Lee patiently listened to a range of bands from Swingin' Blue Jeans, Michael Cox, and Tony Sheridan and the Beatles ("It's a pretty good record," Jerry Lee opined of the latter.

"But it gets a little monotonous about halfway through"), to Bern Eliott and the Fenmen, the Animals, and the Rolling Stones ("one of our top groups and a new outfit" Jerry Lee was dutifully informed). Asked what he thinks about British musicians in general, he answers carefully, no doubt mindful of his audience and of the seismic rumblings beneath his feet: "Well, I used to think that they were a bit wooden, but I've noticed they have more feel for what they are doing now. You have some very fine musicians." He adds, in continent-sized underestimation, "I'm sure that if rock 'n' roll ever gets big again in the world, England will have a lot to do with it."

The day after Jerry Lee's Granada performance, the Beatles released the single "Can't Buy Me Love" (it would spend three weeks at the #1 spot on the U.K. chart) and appeared live on *Ready, Steady, Go!* in front of the program's largest-ever viewing audience, receiving an on-air award from America's *Billboard* magazine, to boot. Jerry Lee Lewis couldn't sigh, or listen glumly to jingling pounds going into others' pockets. He had work to do.

It was 95 miles south to Birmingham Town Hall for the next night's gig, which was by all accounts as uproarious as the Grenada show had been. Green was again dispatched to cover the Killer, and he wrote a week later, "If ever a man earned his pay, Jerry did. He packed more excitement, energy and sheer electrical impact into his eleven numbers than you could find in a shop of LPs." Green breathlessly recapped the show, revealing that Jerry Lee revived a number of crowd-baiting gestures for the Brummies at Town Hall, including sending his piano bench through the air (his roadies were kept busy), "playing" with his foot, and stopping to, as Green put it, "comb his hair as if taunting the teenagers, then [shaking] his hips in a way that made Presley seem an old man." The show built in the same breakneck way to the same wild finish. "It took him almost two minutes to fight his way off-stage at the end of the number," Green writes, "but so great was the acclaim from the audience that after another three minutes, he had to return for an encore ... About twenty boys tried to climb on the platform and Jerry rushed over to them and shook hands with as many as he could reach." When Jerry Lee at last made it to the relative calm of his dressing room, "his shirt was soaked and his hair matted." Appends Green, ever-observant fly on the wall: "He collapsed into a chair and was breathless for minutes."

Though the boys in the venues were the ones who crowded him like knocked-out apostles, Jerry Lee had something special waiting for the girls, those who were brave enough to get near him, anyway. Hours before the Granada recording, he and buddy Cecil Harrelson, accompanied by Jerry Lee's friend Graham Knight, had dashed across Piccadilly Square in the center of Manchester, ducked into a local Lewis department store and, after a bit of Ferriday jocularity, each bought a pair of leopard-skin underpants. "Just wait till the girls see us in these," he grinned.

Who knows how much time he had for carousing, really — the U.K. tour was exhausting. Jerry Lee swallowed hard at the itinerary in his hands: Newcastle; Reading; West Ham Baths; Bloxwich; Glasgow; York; Kingston; Warrington; Liverpool; Coventry; Manchester; Mudeford; London; Bristol; South Harrow; Hereford Hillside — 19 shows in 20 days, a boozy blur of afternoon and evening gigs, festivals, a private house party, a BBC radio performance, long bus rides, sheep and hillsides out of every goddamned window. Each show was well publicized, well attended, and wholly blasted by Jerry Lee. Six years after his marriage scandal, the Southern Wildcat was doing pretty well.

But for record sales, that is. Back home, Singleton and Mercury executives were scratching their heads, ears pivoting to the British sounds pouring from the radio and eyes turned toward the dwindling coffers. The March 21 *Billboard* Hot 100 told the wretched tale: the top three spots belonged to the Beatles ("She Loves You," "I Want To Hold Your Hand," "Please Please Me") who also secured the seventh spot ("Twist and Shout"), their good fortunes spread among four elbowing record labels. Fighting their way in the remaining scrum were the Four Seasons ("Dawn [Go Away]"), the Beach Boys ("Fun, Fun, Fun"), Diane Renay ("Navy Blue"), Al Hirt ("Java"), and Louis Armstrong ("Hello, Dolly!"). The week that Jerry Lee is burning up stages, his commercial state is frigid. Such will remain his dilemma for the next half decade. The Beatles' ironclad, unparalleled mastery of the charts will stay in place for years and will open them to like-minded Mop Toppers, some fantastic, some dreadful, battling their way into the romance, politics, and ever-evolving complexities of the Youth Movement, along with novelty record singers, soaring r&b balladeers, the odd garage band. The Old Guard of rock & roll is just that: decaying and unhip. Jerry Lee couldn't pay the radio to spin his records (and he'd probably tried). The Scouse writing was on the wall. The highest debuting single that week? "We Love You Beatles" by the Carefrees.

What to do? Jerry Lee had a family to support, an incrementally suspicious if dutiful wife to love and placate, a manager, road managers, road crews to pay, a house to remodel, cars to buy, furtive women to wine, dine, and ignore. In short, he had to make bread. He'd continue to hit the road throughout the year and decade, a grueling journey of two-a-day shows, packed or half-empty venues, long, lonely drives, escalating booze and pills, the nightly battle to renew and reinvest himself in what he does and loves the best. It wore. It wears. There was little else to do except maybe retire and become a fisherman down in Louisiana, as he threatened to do to friends and the press in his dark hours. Meanwhile, Beatlemania was *deafening.* Could Jerry Lee hear the piercing screams over the North Sea? Could he picture the dollar signs as fabled twinkling constellations, smell the fickle and trembling, open-mouthed young girls as he made his way to West Germany for the final two shows of the tour?

Philips Records executives had a brilliant idea: the European distributor of Mercury-Smash wanted to record a live album. Considering Jerry Lee "in house" and thus in their jurisdiction, the label folk neglected to inform Shelby Singleton. Jerry Lee and the Nashville Teens were notified before the tour commenced, and an arrangement was secured with the Star-Club in Hamburg, West Germany, a popular venue in a country ripe for American rock & roll. The club possessed an excellent sound system and its own recording deck and crew.

For the past two years, Jerry Lee's reputation as an incendiary performer had only grown wildly, and he'd proven that he was rocking as hard as ever. Why not try to capture that momentum and energy in an album that might sell? It was a bit of a commercial risk: in 1964, the live album market was slim. Stevie Wonder's

Little Stevie Wonder/The 12-Year-Old Genius and James Brown's seminal *Live At The Apollo* had reached #1 and #2 respectively on the pop charts the year before, but it wouldn't be until the end of the decade and into the next that the live album would become a customary artistic release, occasionally selling as well as or greater than studio albums — as would become the case with Peter Frampton, Grand Funk Railroad, Johnny Cash, the Who, Cheap Trick, KISS, *et al.* — and in some cases becoming the album chiefly associated with the performer. The self-mythologizing era of arena- and festival-venue pomp that rock lurched majestically toward in the late 1960s/early 1970s would make grandiose, "event"-live albums fashionable (think Elvis Presley's *Aloha from Hawaii Via Satellite*). But in 1964, with jazz and blues exceptions, live records were rare, especially in the American market, and were often lamely recorded and/or cooked-up in a studio. George Martin recorded the Beatles at the Hollywood Bowl in 1964 and 1965, but urged Capital Records to shelve the album because of poor sound quality; Chess Records released *Chuck Berry On Stage* in 1963, but a swift inspection would reveal overdubbed crowd applause and screams; the Rolling Stones released *Got Live If You Want It* in 1966, but only after sweetening the tracks, dropping in studio cuts, and adding canned applause where necessary. "We are uncapturable live," Keith Richards admits. "You gotta be there. The funny thing is, when you know you're recording, you can always guarantee that the Stones will not deliver. It's typically perverse." When the Rolling Stones released *Get Yer Ya-Ya's Out* in 1970, there had already been notorious bootlegs from the same tour circulating with allegedly better sound, performances, and vibe.

Live recordings in the early 1960s didn't sell particularly well; for every Wonder or Brown, there was *In Concert at Pacoima Jr. High* by Ritchie Valens. Bo Diddley's fierce *Bo Diddley's Beach Party* from 1963, another early live rock & roll recording — and one of the greatest — didn't even chart. Chess Records possessed one of the first remote recording units of the era, and the raw, primitive mono recording of a July 4th weekend's worth of shows in Myrtle Beach, South Carolina catches the stomping, trance-like momentum of Bo in front of 2,000 raucous fans. But it wasn't exactly radio-friendly stuff. "It generates excitement that only a live recording can," someone promised in the liner notes hopefully, and truthfully. But America wasn't ready for such a primal record. Would they be ready for the Killer?

Translating the live experience is a chancy proposition. The striking stage lighting, the smell of sweat and bodies, the stiff neck, the flirty glances, the anonymous pressing of bodies between stirred-up strangers — these are crucial ingredients in a fun night out watching a band. Blend in beer or vodka, fatigue or adrenaline, the personal or political dramas braiding any group of music-besotted friends and strangers, and you've got an emotional, dimensional encounter that registers far beyond a set-list. How to bring that home in a recording?

Driving back from shows with friends during college — ears ringing, clothes soaked with perspiration, warm Schaefer beer to be downed during the ride back — I knew that what I'd experienced could never be repeated. I might hear a bootleg later, or even crudely that very night through a handheld tape recorder smuggled into the club, but the sounds coming though the speaker would bear little resemblance to what I remembered. I might think *Oh yeah!* to certain songs, certain comments from the stage or from fans around me, but missing was mood, sweat, reverb in the bone marrow. As the ringing in my ears faded (sometimes over a long, scary week, as was the case when I showed up too late at a Ramones show in Baltimore and had to stand next to their Marshall amps) the loss is compounded by something else, the gloomy, fading tattoo of memory.

December, 1981. The Rolling Stones were out supporting *Tattoo You.* Their three-show stand at Capital Center was their first appearance in the Washington, D.C. area in years, and there was immense buzz in the town and on local radio. This would be my first rock show, the first of only two arena shows that I would attend — the Who would come a couple months later, and then the discovery of indie rock and the happy glide into decades of innumerable small-club and theater shows.

Seeing the Stones was intense: snaking onto the floor with a golden ticket, heart pounding, looking back at the bowl seats diminishing upward into smoke; standing in the second row feeling giddily older than I was, eye-popping at the girls in their feathered hair and eyeliner and tight, tongue-wagging Stones jerseys, breathing in perfume and perspiring excitement mingling with the pot, cigarette, and booze haze: *wow*, I was in love with rock & roll. We'd heard that the Stones technicians were jokingly downing the houselights two or three times before the show would start — and though I knew that the trick was coming, every time Capital Center was plunged into darkness, the roar that moved through me as nerve and wind made me light-headed with exhilaration, and not a little good fear. I was contact-high on everything. (Bobby

Womack opened up and I remember not a thing, so amped was I for the Stones.) When the house lights went down for good, the stage began to revolve slowly and the opening notes of "Under My Thumb" came booming across the arena. Keith Richards in his stovepipe jeans and torn, leopard-skin t-shirt, drinking straight from a bottle of Jack Daniels, Mick Jagger's candy-colored football pants, Charlie Watts' studied cool. Clichés all, yes, but all clichés originate in truth. My brother Phil shook Bill Wyman's hand when Wyman ventured out onto a tiny catwalk off of the stage, and flesh-on-flesh exchange, however orchestrated or corny, goes a long way toward dispersing the formulaic.

A weird thing happened in the midst of all of the fun. At some point during the show, Jagger briefly disappeared and emerged in a cherry-picker cage which was then vaulted off of the stage, swinging him out and over the first dozen or so rows. There was a basket of roses in the cage, and Mick was throwing them out at the crowd by the fistful — good, cheesy theatrics, enabling Jagger to be both within and without (a pretty fair approximation of his personality, likely). The cherry-picker swung pretty close to me at one point, and I looked up and got a momentary but very clear glimpse of Jagger: he was so close that I could see the makeup caked on his face, sweat running down in rivulets. His eyes looked bored, elsewhere, dead, a complete and utter jadedness so sincere and shocking that it became as ineffaceable a memory of that show as Richards and Wood trading riffs, maybe more so.

As it turns out, that show was being recorded. *Still Life* appeared the next year, and a couple of the tracks ("Twenty Flight Rock" and "Going To A Go-Go") were taken from the show that I attended. The album is slick and lifeless and, apart from the frisson I still experience every time I listen to "Under My Thumb," sounds very little like what I remember, which was rawer, denser, and, of course, louder. Until a live album, in its analog waves or digital ones and twos, can replicate tinnitus or a chest full of illicit smoke or the helpless urge to grope the painted-on Jordache ass of the girl standing in front of you, a live album risks failure. Could there have been a way to accurately translate Jagger's sighing, uninterested countenance as he flew over my head?

I saw Government Issue at the Atrium Room in the Student Union at the University of Maryland, in the mid-1980s. I looked up at the glass-paneled ceiling, transfixed, watching the maelstrom of the mosh pit in front of me reflected in all of its insanity, fear, and glory. How is that story retold in audio? When the Fleshtones end a show by leaving through the club's front door onto the sidewalk and boarding a city bus because it happens to be pulling up at that moment, that's as much a part of their show as the song disappearing when their wireless guitars go out of range down the block. How is that replicated in digital bits? Anyone who's seen Iggy Pop's infamous "crowd walk" from the Stooges' show in Cincinnati in 1970 won't forget it — manifested in the still-shot of Iggy standing, supported by arms and hands in the crowd, while he ominously points off into the distance. Luckily, we have the grainy video of that intense and essential rock & roll moment. Everyone has shows they attended that they can't imagine being accurately reproduced on CD. (For me it was the New Bomb Turks at the Union in Athens, Ohio; Reverend Horton Heat in Chicago at the Hideout; an insane show by the long-gone Oysters at the 9:30 Club in the mid-1980s that I still recall as a miracle of chaos and fun. I caught the Mooney Suzuki at CBGB in Manhattan in 2001. The show has been issued on CD, but I've resisted listening, mildly afraid that my buddies' and my great time had as much to do with the palpable history of the storied venue and the sweaty, grinning Budweisers in our hands as with the performance itself.)

Despite these rather impossible complaints, some of my favorite music memories involve live recordings. In the Seventies my younger brother and I wore out the grooves of KISS' *Alive!*; Pat Travers' exciting call-and-response "Boom Boom (Out Go The Lights)" was in regular rotation on DC101 while I was in training for puberty. Shortly after the Stones show, I happened across J. Geils Band's *"Live" Full House.* I knew and had liked their "Love Stinks" radio hit, but had heard that their earlier stuff was better, rocked harder. *Full House* was — is — a great rock & roll album, strikingly capturing the ambience of Detroit's Cinderella Hall and the tight swagger of the band, their strutting r&b really riling up a rabid crowd. As critic Tim Sendra puts it, the music on *Full House* "jumps out of the speakers with so much joy, fun, and unquenchable rock & roll spirit that you might as well be there." Yes: I could nearly smell the venue, and Detroit in the early 1970s felt grimy and exhilarating.

The MC5 released a live album as their debut in 1969, and the two songs that open *Kick Out The Jams* remain among the most exciting blasts of live rock & roll ever recorded (and call back to Bo Diddley's exhortations on his *Beach Party* album from six years earlier). As recorded by Bruce Botnick, the atmosphere of Detroit's Grande Ballroom nearly seeps from the tracks, and the blend of the band's raw-throated politics, the songs' sonic hugeness, and the crowd's excitement is palpable and heady so many years later. The same can be said of the opening trio of songs on the Ramones' *It's Alive* from 1979: if you could listen to only three songs from the Kings of Queens it might as well be these three, which capture in six minutes all you need to know about the band, their audience, American punk, and where rock & roll had to go after blowing up the excess and pomposity of much of the 1970s. Over the years, some live performances have lodged themselves among my favorite songs, such as the Jam's "Down In The Tube Station At Midnight," a b-side from 1980 that's shatteringly fierce — the last 90 seconds in particular — an obscure highlight of the post-punk era.

One particular track has become for me a kind of talisman. I knew the Flamin' Groovies' "Shake Some Action" from WHFS, the great progressive radio station in Bethesda, Maryland, where afternoon dj Weasel would often play it. A majestic pop anthem, the song is one of my favorites, an example of the power and desperate sincerity in a great, three-minute pop song. Sometime in high school, my brother Phil's friend Jim introduced me to another version of the song, a live recording by Charlie Pickett and the Eggs. (Jim had put the version on an ironic mix-tape he made that he called the *Death Tape*: every song on it was so good and so intense that listening to it while driving could have lethal results. I think that the Modern Lovers' "Roadrunner" was on there, and Jim Carroll's "People Who Died," and J. Geils Band's "Looking For A Love" from *"Live" Full House*. This was the mid-1980s and blow was everywhere and, looking back, the *Death Tape* was a native element in those speedy, reckless years: lines in the backseat of someone's '72 Toyota in the Tastee Diner parking lot, a sluggish, beery evening ignited afresh.

Jim had an apartment on upper Connecticut Avenue in Northwest Washington, D.C., and these were fun nights ending with rock & roll on the stereo and the chalky, electrifying taste of cocaine in the backs of throats.)

Charlie Pickett and the Eggs' version of "Shake Some Action" is remarkable. Like so much of the best rock & roll, it threatens to fall apart at each measure. It's sloppy, anthemic, authentic, and frightening. Near the end of the first chorus, someone at the Button — the got-to-be-tacky club in Fort Lauderdale, Florida, where the show was recorded in January of 1982 — lets loose a barely audible whoop of pleasure or pain or rhapsody or torture; it's hard to know which exactly, but it's spine-tingling in its weirdness. As I remember, this was Jim's favorite moment. We'd guffaw while we listened, drunk and zooming, the tops of our heads coming off at the song's oddly stirring desperation. *Live At The Button* is a great record, well-recorded and full of loose and shoddy bar-band rock & roll, a couple of Pickett originals and some other great covers, like the Flamin' Groovies' "Slow Death," in front of a drunk and rowdy crowd. "Shake Some Action" was the highlight and still remains one of the high points in my music collection: proof that a venue's ambience — in which both song and crowd fuse into something combustible — can be translated by audio somehow, perhaps only by magic and luck. The guy who sold the album to me was a record store owner in Fort Lauderdale who was not only at the Pickett show, but claims to remember that other-worldly howl during "Shake Some Action." I believe him.

When I was eight or nine, my brothers took me up to Variety Records in Wheaton Plaza where the owners were showing a rare video copy of the Beatles playing at Shea Stadium in 1965. I remember being part of a small but buzzing crowd. The Beatles jogged out of the dugout and onto the playing field — the stadium was only a year old at the time, and must've felt as state-of-the-art new as did the Beatles' music — and thousands of flashbulbs popped and the screams descended as wraithlike, fabled waves of white noise, and I was overwhelmed at the images and the sensations, and found them impossible to describe. Like the moment when the front door opened at the old 9:30 Club in Washington, D.C., through that sliver coming a momentary roar of music and smells and mood and heart-tensing sensation.

"Jerry Lee was and is a very talented person. The damned problem was figuring out how to capture that talent," Shelby Singleton once lamented.

After an appearance at a festival in Hillside, England, Jerry Lee dried himself off, combed back his hair, boarded Japanese Air Lines and with the Nashville Teens flew across the North Sea to West Berlin. On April 4 they played at the massive Deutschlandhalle, at that time Europe's largest indoor performance venue. Built in 1936, the hall was sizeable enough to host Olympic events and the world's first indoor test-flight as well as large-scale music performances (in 1960 Ella Fitzgerald released an album recorded there, the widely hailed *Ella In Berlin*), but its bulk couldn't defend the onslaught of brutal air-raids during the second war. Deutschlandhalle was considerably rebuilt and re-branded in the late 1950s, and Jerry Lee was pleased to have sold out the now thriving venue in a show promoted by the Star-Club and featuring in support slots King Size Taylor & the Dominoes, the Phantom Brothers, and Johnny & the Hurricanes. He played a long, well-received set to a standing-room-only crowd of thousands;

backstage, killing time and obviously enjoying himself, he busked some blues and country & western classics for the fellow musicians. The next day, he settled back for the 290-kilometer flight northwest to Hamburg.

The last of the important St. Pauli "Beat Clubs," the Star-Club opened on April 13, 1962. When electrician, establishment owner, and Reeperbahn fixture Manfred Weissleder began looking for another venue to own and manage, he turned his attention to the *Stern Kino* — the Star Cinema — a run-down adult movie theater at Grosse Freiheit 39. Aiming high from the onset and sinking not an inconsiderable amount of his own money into the venture, Weissleder wanted not merely to compete with the nearby and wildly popular Top Ten Club, but to blind it with the star power that he would bring to his new joint, which in deference to its former name he dubbed the Star-Club.

With uber-bouncer-cum-manager Horst Fascher at the door, traversing the interior when necessary to sort out the drunken melees, glad-handing the local organized element, and shining his considerable and muscled magnetism, the Star-Club opened to great success. In his book *Let The Good Times Roll!* Fascher describes the crowd on opening night, which began with a near-empty Grosse Freiheit but ended triumphantly with a packed house: "This was what they had been waiting for all this time," he marveled. "And now they were shouting out their impatience, their boisterous joy. On the dance floor people were squeezed into a pulsating mass. Still they were able to dance. No one sat. They were applauding, singing along, or stamping their feet."

The Star-Club was soon renowned along the

Reeperbahn. At its most successful, the venue would
feature rotating one-hour sets by up to eight bands a day,
from the legendary to the obscure. The Beatles, of course,
opened the club to that pulsating crowd in 1962 and
would play five engagements there, honing their chops,
building their stamina, and losing their innocence; by
the end of their last residency they were mere weeks away
from superstardom. Other British acts played regularly
and for years there, including the aforementioned King
Size Taylor & the Dominoes, Tony Sheridan, Ian and the
Zodiacs, the Remo Four, Lee Curtis & the All Stars, the
all-girl Liverbirds, and many others.

What made the Star-Club unique in St. Pauli, however, was its roster of American rock & roll and r&b stars,
who were attracted as much by the venue's storied sound
system and well-managed air of respectability — such
as it was in the vibrant and violent Kiel red-light district
— as by the fervent German taste for American music
and the all-night "amusements" along the Reeperbahn.
(Depending on one's personal style, orientation, or marital status, the friendly and generous maidens who worked
those establishments and walked those blocks only added
to the Star-Club's charm.) Fats Domino, Chuck Berry,
Gene Vincent, Little Richard, the Everly Brothers, Bo
Diddley, Joey Dee & the Starliters, and Ray Charles would
all play the Star-Club before its close in 1969, their names
emblazoned on the iconic marquee arching over the
entrance under which walked thousands of Germans,
visiting Europeans, and American servicemen eager for
a rum-and-coke or lager-fueled night of loud bands
that would *mach schau* until dawn. Nearby clubs were
ultimately crippled by the Star-Club's might: "A desperate
tactic of the less wealthy Top Ten," Alan Clayson relates,

"was to bill a Glaswegian duo who xeroxed the Everly Brothers as the real thing for two months while the *real* real thing managed only four evenings at the Star-Club."

Loud, primitive rock & roll was still raising eyebrows and concerns among some social commentators. After witnessing a 1963 Jerry Lee performance at the Star-Club, journalist Werner Sillescu wrote a nervous article in the daily *Hamburger Abendblatt* attempting "to give an impression of this phenomenon," wherein he augustly wondered, "Can artificially generated, organized noise be relaxing? Is it an alternative to the noise we unfortunately call progress? Furthermore: is a mild form of rhythmic ecstasy possible and useful in our civilized order? We must ask ourselves these questions nowadays, as the Star Club begins to gather steam like a boiling cauldron."

Sillescu's commentary is a fascinating, time-capsule admonition against the primal energies let loose in the Star-Club, and by extension along the Reeperbahn, through St. Pauli, and into the hearts and groins of German youths via rock *und* roll. "The noise crouches in the dark room like a daunting animal that attacks those who enter with a crushing impact," Sillescu writes. "It hits them hard in the stomach, and is brutal to the eardrum and every nerve. The noise is rhythmically pounding, as in a factory full of machines. But this is no factory. It is a former theater, in which rock & roll and the twist now reign. With time, the ear distinguishes voices out of the pounding, rhythmic shreds of melody. The eye recognizes tables, chairs, a well-lit stage with a very decorative sky-scraper backdrop, and young people. They sit and stand tightly packed. The dance floor is so full there's no room for even a mouse to squeeze in." It's "star night," and the star is Jerry Lee Lewis. "The regular radio-listener will not have heard this name yet," Sillecsu reassures his readers. "For the fans, however, he is as good as gold."

In detached, anthropological fashion, Sillescu surveys and describes the Star-Club's clientele: machinists, trainees, industrial apprentices, harbor workers, "simple, unpretentious, and strong. They are the same ones who besiege the Reeperbahn from atop the cathedral. Preferred clothing is the leather jacket. Some with, some without a tie. The clothing doesn't really make any difference. What's comfortable is what's allowed: jeans, sweaters, t-shirts. Long hair is piled up with heavy amounts of pomade and carefully crossed at the neck." Girls are not seen often, Sillescu notes. "They really aren't needed; you can do the twist by yourself. There is no sense of the erotic. The stage is a parquet of mirrors. The same type of person that dominates the audience is found on the stage as well, but these are armed with electric guitars and percussion instruments."

The music, Sillescu frowns, "consists solely of rhythm. Even the most discerning of ears can discover no cohesive melody. If a melody were there, it would have been utterly drowned out by the droning rhythm." But none of this matters. "It's all about rhythm here. It's primitive, stomped out in two-stroke beats, with a triplet played over it, grating against the beat and creating excitement. The audience contributes to the melody, assimilates it, and is carried away by it. The guys stamp their feet, clap, keep the beat with their arms, and entwine themselves in the steps of the twist. They somehow find room for all of this, despite the overcrowded dance floor."

And then the Killer appears. "The sea of fans receive him with cheering, whistling, stomping — with an orgy of noise," Sillescu reports. "The cult-crowd goes wild before the star has issued a single note. It's a thing of ritual. The star, pale, in a dark stage tuxedo, sits at the piano and hammers out the same chord, in rhythm with the band, for several minutes. He heats his audience up before he takes the microphone and sings something that no one can understand. The guys and girls in the room go wild; they lose themselves in the rhythm and in their excitement. Only when they feel like they're being watched do they settle down and become embarrassed. The boiling cauldron bubbles ever wilder, and suddenly unstable-looking figures appear on a level above everyone else — sitting on their friends' shoulders. Up there they scream and wave their arms shakily to the beat. One takes off his pullover in excitement and swings it through the air; an outside observer would be easily unsettled."

Shuddering, Sillescu wonders, "What kind of pent-up cases are these people, letting loose in rhythmical ecstasy? Specifically, only simple folk respond to this form of rhythm. It leaves the pretentious intellect cold."

The alarmed editorial concludes with a rather transparent attempt at dumbing-down rock & roll by presenting "the star" backstage, "composed" but "almost arrogant." The star is asked whether or not he has thought about the deeper causes of the bewildering effect of his music. "He gives a blank stare," Sillescu helpfully reports. "He hasn't. It's also not to be expected. He's cut from the same wood as the stage itself. The star and his fans understand each other on an emotional level. Whoever tries to think too much about it automatically breaks the connection of the electrical circuit between star and fan."

Sillescu sighs, "Perhaps psychologists and sociologists will find an explanation for what goes on at the Star Club.

The normal citizen can only marvel." Jerry Lee was back for his second spin of the place, hot from riotous shows in England, prepared to astonish the *normale Bürgers*. And Philips was going to get it all down on tape.

A fair-haired, soft-spoken jazz man, he had catholic taste and a commercial ear. And Siggi Loch sensed the tremors of something new in northern Germany.

"I was the head of the jazz department at Philips Records," Loch says. "But I was also very interested in blues and rhythm & blues, and so this brought me to the Star-Club to see Fats Domino and Chuck Berry. It was great. And of course I realized that there were all of these young, mainly British, bands who were playing Chuck Berry and other white American rock & rollers, their big heroes. I thought, *Hey, there's a new kind of music developing here.* And I went to the owner and made a proposal to start recording the bands at the Star-Club, which I did." Loch's initial recordings were successful, and led to the establishment of Star-Club Records, a small regional label distributed by Philips; common to the releases was Loch's working relationship with sturdy engineers, in particular Peter Krampre ("a genius," says Loch), and their co-commitment to audio fidelity. More than three decades later, after being assigned a handful of Loch's mid-1960s recordings to master, esteemed American engineer Greg Calbi told Loch that the tapes were brilliant and that he couldn't do a thing to them, such were their high fidelity and worth. Calbi simply transferred and digitized them, leaving them essentially as they were.

Loch and Krampre's setup for Jerry Lee was of the era, and characteristically uncomplicated: mike Jerry Lee, mike the band, mike the audience, get the tapes rolling — trusting by necessity that the simple recording would adequately capture the band's performance and the crowd's reactions. "All of the stuff that we recorded in those days were two-track stereo direct to quarter-inch tape, we had no multi-track recording facility," Loch explains. "We positioned the mike as close as possible to the instruments, and then placed a stereo mike in the audience to capture the ambience." When engineer Bill Inglott was called upon to master the Star-Club tapes for release 30 years later, he was astonished by how little work he had to do. "We used the original master that was delivered to Mercury U.S.A. in the 1960s," Inglott says. "We spent all of three hours mastering it." He adds, "When the recordings and performance are that great, there's not much to do."

Says Loch now: "I think it's one of the most electrifying rock & roll shows ever recorded."

Weissleder had wholly renovated the large Star-Club, keeping only an upstairs balcony from the original cinema floor plan. Outside, he highlighted the address in a neon starburst next to a lurid sign spelling out E-R-O-T-I-C; inside he installed two sizeable bars, one in the balcony and one along the back wall, a trellis-festooned drop-ceiling hung with lanterns to heighten the illusion of intimacy, painted a poor-man's Manhattan skyline across the back wall, and stocked the floor with tables and chairs, many of which, when a star of Jerry Lee's caliber was performing, would be removed to increase the paid attendance. "The people were really pushed in, and you could hardly breathe," Loch remembers of those nights. "Thank god that there was never an accident, because it would have been fatal." For Jerry Lee's April 5 engagement, a sparkle-striped grand piano with Roman winged-griffon detailing was wheeled in and positioned, from the audience's perspective, on the right side of the stage, allowing ample room for the backing band to set up and for the Killer to roam, if he felt the need.

The Nashville Teens formed in 1962 in Surrey, England. While backing Jerry Lee on the three-week tour they were anxiously awaiting their debut single, "Tobacco Road," an exciting number that would eventually reach #6 and #14 on the British and American singles charts, respectively. The Teens uniquely sported two lead singers, Arthur Sharp and Ray Phillips, but the lineup that supported Jerry Lee in the U.K. and Germany was a lean trio: Pete Shannon Harris on bass, John Allen on guitar, and Barrie Jenkins on drums. Keyboard player John Hawken naturally stepped out of the way of the Killer storm-front, and with Sharp and Phillips watched the mania mostly from the wings. "Being one of the few bands with a piano player, we played a lot of Jerry Lee Lewis material," Hawken remembers. "Don Arden, who became our manager just prior to the Jerry Lee Lewis tour, realized this and thought we'd be the ideal band to back him. Jerry Lee used my piano pick-ups which were more powerful than his own. They'd been specially made for me by Roger Mayer, an electronics whiz who made all sorts of effect boxes and gadgets later for people like Jimi Hendrix and Jimmy Page."

Hawken recalls the Star-Club fondly. "It was a great venue to play, with a usually large and enthusiastic crowd which would constantly change as the night wore on until there'd be only a handful of sullen drunks hanging around at the very end, around 3 or 4 a.m." The Nashville Teens, like so many English bands before and after them, had gotten into fighting shape in Hamburg, packing on musical muscle and mettle with long nights of long sets in front of hoarse and at times volatile crowds. By the time they were performing their own sets and setting up behind Jerry Lee, they were a sharp, tight r&b outfit. Need proof? Listen to the great, driving "Tobacco Road" and the stomping rhythm bed provided by Harris and Jenkins, the stop-start groove leading deliriously into a sing-along chorus sprinkled with double-time piano fills; Hawken had indeed been listening to plenty of Jerry Lee's Sun records.

Each member of the Nashville Teens was paid a one-off fee of £18 — but how much money could prepare and soothe the wounds of a band playing for the first time behind the Killer? A notoriously difficult musician with whom to work, Jerry Lee leads with his considerable chops and oversized personality, leaving vulnerable backing musicians in his wake, especially if they're new to him. Before the Granada television show, the Nashville Teens had had a disagreement with Jerry Lee, the details of which are lost to time, and the resulting squabble led to the Flintstones backing him on that program. He relented afterwards and, save for a few gigs where the Flintstones provided support, the Teens set up behind him — much to their pleasure, as they loved the tour's packed houses. But the circuit was not without some unhappy, tense moments, mostly onstage where the Killer is in charge and the center of attention, where anything or anyone who interferes with that attention might face the Ferriday wrath. "He was always very much the star and expected us to follow his lead at all times," bassist Pete Harris acknowledges. "His performances were unscripted, there was no list of numbers to be played. He rarely introduced the songs by name. He just started playing the new number on his own and we had to recognize which one and in which key, and then join in."

Such recklessness might've been murder on the band, but the fearlessness with which they were forced to leap in increases the energy level and wildness of the performances. "He did have a tendency to speed up through numbers," Harris adds, "particularly when he did the piano solo, and it was very difficult for Barrie and I to hold him back. This is what happened on the Star-Club recording." Often irritable, and conscious of his own onstage importance, Jerry Lee wouldn't refrain from lecturing his backing band if he felt that they were dragging. A kind of pathology, maybe, and an adolescent way of keeping control and power; it also contributes to the rock & roll spirit in Jerry Lee Lewis' best live recordings. "I think it was mainly his stage ego that was the problem, as he was quite pleasant to talk to on occasions off stage," Harris reflects. "He must have accepted that the Nashville Teens were a competent backing group despite us being rhythm & blues orientated, as opposed to rock & roll, otherwise he would not have put up with us."

Harris particularly remembers one public dressing-down. "We played a gig at Leyton Town Baths, now probably demolished, in London when I failed to guess correctly the key of the number he had started to play. During the number, whilst John Allen was doing the guitar solo, Jerry Lee walked across the stage to me, followed by the spotlight, wagged his finger at me and shouted: 'The key is E-F-F, man!'" Duly noted, Killer.

Hamburg was enjoying pleasantly cool April weather when Jerry Lee arrived in the afternoon, the Reeperbahn already buzzing. He settled into his favorite hotel in the district, on Lincolnstraße, and likely gazed out the window with a blend of fascination and caution. "He insisted on living in St. Pauli," Horst Fascher remembers. "He wanted to be 'in the middle of the excitement, there, where life plays its dirtiest game,' he told me." The Star-Club gig was the last show of the tour, and Jerry Lee had nothing to do but soak up the city, drink a bit, and let it rip.

He got to the club early. After sets from afternoon bands the Giants and King Size Taylor & the Dominoes, he rendezvoused with the Nashville Teens for a sound check and to allow Loch and Krampre to set up the mikes and confirm sound-balances for the recording. During a lull before the ticketed crowd was allowed in, Jerry Lee sat at the piano and played a handful of country & western and gospel spiritual numbers as members of the Nashville Teens and the Giants watched and listened in rapt attention. "This was of the highest standard, no histrionics or stagecraft, just pure music," Pete Harris remembers fondly. "Wonderful." Sadly, the busking wasn't recorded for posterity; for the lucky few who were there, Jerry Lee had reached into his weathered bag of standards and regional classics, his self-consciousness at bay, his stage ego for the moment supplanted by a pure gesture of playing music at the piano in the simple, devotional act that it has always been for him.

Afterward, everyone reassembled in the spacious dressing room where the drinking and friendly conversations reignited. After the crowd were let in, the Nashville Teens hit the stage, opened the first set, and were very well received. Though 9 p.m. was fairly early in the evening by Reeperbahn standards, the crowd was already well lubricated, the whiskey, rum, and beers flowing as plentifully as the Elbe. After a short break, an announcement came over the PA that the night's show was being recorded for a live album, and Jerry Lee strode from the wings to thunderous applause. He wore a dark pin-stripe suit jacket and dark flannel pants, white shirt and dark tie, black striped socks, and pointed black-leather shoes. Hair sufficiently harnessed. He grinned at the crowd, knowing that they'd barely understand a goddamned word he'd say all night, and took a seat on the piano bench. Behind him, Pete Harris, John Allen, and Barrie Jenkins sat eager and tense at their instruments, waiting for their cue.

The History

The first set was comprised of "Down the Line," "You Win Again," "High School Confidential," "Your Cheatin' Heart," "Great Balls Of Fire," "What'd I Say, Parts 1 & 2," and "Mean Woman Blues." A two-hour intermission followed while Jerry Lee toweled off and sipped some whiskey; Horst-Dieter Fischer, then president of the German fan club, remembers Jerry Lee — stuck by the purity of his earlier solo piano playing to a half-empty club — shaking off the rock & roll excess and again reaching toward his restorative roots, this time via an acoustic guitar that someone had tossed his way. "He started strumming and picking it," Fisher recalls. "He sang and played guitar to songs like 'Hi-Heel Sneakers,' 'Twist and Shout,' some country tunes and, most surprisingly, quite a lot of old and rather unknown blues songs." The private performance was so surprising and startling that Loch urged Jerry Lee to do some of the blues tunes during his second set, just him singing and playing guitar onstage. But he refused, telling Siggi that he knew that the audience had come to see him sing and pound rock

& roll on the piano. Laments Fischer: "I know we missed something that night." Jerry Lee shrugged, put the guitar down, strolled back onstage to an even wilder reception, stretched his fingers, cocked a half-grin, rechanneled the Killer, and played a frantic second set of "Good Golly Miss Molly," "Matchbox," "Money," "Whole Lotta Shakin' Goin' On," "Lewis Boogie," "Hound Dog," "Long Tall Sally," and "I'm On Fire."

The History, Rewritten

From those 16 songs, Siggi Loch created one of the great rock & roll albums of all time, *created* being the operative term: in addition to producing, Loch was responsible for selecting the final running order for the album. I'll admit that I was surprised and a bit disappointed when I learned that *"Live" At The Star-Club* is a compilation of two sets, that the performances I'd loved and known for so many years had been spliced together — but as every fan of live albums knows, track sequencing is where much of the magic occurs. In creating an ersatz set, alternating tracks, cocking an ear to tempo and mood, Loch arranged an album — an experience — that built, swelled, and exhaled over the course of two sides. If not a technically accurate document of Jerry Lee Lewis on the night of April 5, 1964, *"Live" At The Star-Club* has rightly become that evening's holy writ.

What the shuffling of tracks couldn't fake was the atmosphere at the club, as much an attraction that night as Jerry Lee's playing or the Nashville Teens' muscular support. Loch and Krampre capture the venue's feel with tactile aplomb. Trevor Duplock was a member of the aforementioned Giants, an English band from Brighton that was playing a month-long engagement at the Star-Club when Jerry Lee arrived. Duplock, whose band was also a veteran of the famed Cavern Club in Liverpool, England, remembers the aura of the club and the surrounding area well, the Reeperbahn having dazzled him as it had so many wide-eyed youths: "Twenty-four hour bars, all-night music clubs, strip joints, gangsters, legalized prostitution. They even had a club across the street from the Star-Club that had naked female wrestling! Outside every bar and club, men in military-looking uniforms and hats trying to entice you inside. I loved walking around there at night, truly, truly amazing. And in the midst of this astonishing place is what many regarded as the greatest rock & roll club on earth." An 18-year-old in 1964, Duplock was among the youngest musicians playing the Star-Club then, and he and fellow Giants drummer John Hills were forced to apply for special work permits, such was the notoriety of the Reeperbahn. "The two of us had to report to a local police station every week so that the police could check that we were OK, and not being corrupted!" Duplock laughs. "How do you corrupt a rock musician?"

The mood and tangible atmosphere of the Star-Club hit Duplock the moment he set foot inside. "It was the kind of audience you pray for as a performer. A rock riot every night, wonderful dancing. The best rock music you could hear anywhere on the planet, played by some of the most accomplished rock musicians around. The Star-Club was a rock music Citadel." John Hills might add that the fortress demanded exceptionally hard work of its employees. "The club opened at 6 p.m. and played through the night until 6 a.m. the following day," Hills says. "All of the bands took three one-hour spots, scattered on a duty rotated throughout the night. If you were really unlucky, you could find yourself first on with another spot at around midnight and then having to stay right to the end for the lonely last spot."

Exhaustion aside, Hills, Duplock and the other musicians were keyed up to see Jerry Lee. His appearance had been billed and promoted well in advance, the evening's kick echoed and exaggerated in the great buzz of neon signs and long, splayed legs along the Reeperbahn. The show sold out quickly — the day of the show the line went up the street and around the corner, with hundreds of more people anxious to get a ticket — and the club was packed from the moment it opened at midday. "You needed a special ticket for the evening show, the time of the Jerry Lee recording, but everyone was hoping to sneak past or around that ruling by getting in early," says Duplock. "Half of Hamburg seemed to be there. I must have been asked a hundred times that day if I could get tickets or get someone in. It was one gigantic party." When the Giants played the club, their usual haunt between sets was a small bar next to the club, "but when Jerry Lee was playing it was so packed I couldn't even get near it. Trying to move around inside was totally impossible."

The Giants played a late-afternoon show with the Dominoes. "Coming up to five in the afternoon, it was just going crazy," Duplock remembers. "We were just about to go on, the Dominoes were, as usual, roaring to a finish, just one hour to go. The last hour flew by. We played our set, closed with 'Lucille.' Our usual big finish number, some of the local guys used to stand and bang their heads against the front edge of the stage when we did that song. In time with the beat! I often wonder if the phrase 'Headbangers' originated from the audience at the Star-Club. Some of those guys were totally crazy."

Following the Giants' set, those on the floor without tickets were unceremoniously booted, and the club was emptied; after soundcheck, those with tickets and those fortunate enough to have been invited by the bands and local cognoscenti swarmed the club. This was not a typical rock & roll crowd. Lining the front of the shoulder-high stage were the hardcore, greased-up Rockers, already trashed, foaming, pounding the stage, determined to get as close as possible to the Killer. Behind them roiled an age- and class-blended group of those hoping to dance, mostly beehive-coifed German girls and their boyfriends and club regulars, Americans and British who'd come from the local Air Force and Army bases, a back bar crowded with folks craning their necks for a view of the stage, and a small group of tables set out at the back of the standing area and in front of the bar occupied by Hamburg glitterati. "Friends of the owner, probably one or two gangsters," Duplock recalls. "Women in long dresses dripping in diamonds next to rockers dressed head to toe in black. Fantastic audience." Into this scene strutted the Killer.

As sequenced by Loch, *"Live" At The Star-Club* begins with rolling l's tossed at the riotous crowd, in Jerry Lee's typically lubricious, come-on way. As Jimmy Gutterman puts it: "He did not wait for the opening number to start performing." The trio of songs that opens *"Live" At The Star-Club* are so gargantuan, so impossibly rocking and intense, that it's a wonder that the listener survives them. They call to my mind the opening salvo of the MC5's *Kick Out The Jams* and the Ramones' *It's Alive* — breakneck, barely controlled, scary — and are among the greatest rock & roll ever taped.

Perhaps Jerry Lee ratcheted things up because it was

the last night of the tour, and because he knew that the show was being recorded. Or perhaps, stinging from his polite performance in front of Richard Green in the *New Musical Express* offices a few weeks earlier, he was psyched to do American music proud in the face of this longhaired Limey nonsense ("I used to think that they were a bit wooden . . ."). Perhaps the Prellies that Fascher remembers Jerry Lee extravagantly downing nightly with whiskey chasers amped up his native speed, leaving the Nashville Teens coughing in his exhaust. Perhaps we're simply lucky that this particular show in April was recorded.

When the lights come down and the emcee bellows "Jerry Lee Lewis!" to a cacophony of cheers, whistles, and clapping, we're transported into the loud, smoky Grosse Freiheit 39 on a rowdy Saturday night. Loch's crowd microphone and the subsequent mix tap the cries, hollers, cheers, and sometimes stray conversations of the large crowd, surely as essential an ingredient of the album's triumph as the performances. Horst-Dieter Fischer recalls that before the second set, folks were asked to leave the dance floor and to sit down at the tables and at the bars, to eliminate audience noise from the recordings. The well-intentioned effort failed, thankfully. The crowd at the Star-Club on this evening doesn't hide, muffled, behind a soundboard veil — everyone's around you, behind you, elbowing, glad-handing, throwing their collective inebriated arm around you. Who needs Steinhagers or *rum und koks*? *"Live" At The Star-Club* is the only album I know that can get you drunk even if there's no alcohol in your house.

"Thank you, thank you very much ladies and gentleman. I'd like to say it's a pleasure, a great honor, to be back at the fabulous, most beautiful, I mean really swingin' Star-Club. Yeah!"

"Mean Woman Blues," the lead cut, is nothing short of a mini concert in and of itself. Loch chose well: Jerry Lee had released a version of Claude Demetrius' song on an EP in 1957, a few months after Elvis Presley had issued his own take (on the *Loving You* film soundtrack). Elvis' version was fun, swinging, and pretty dirty for the late 1950s, and he clearly has fun taking the risk. Jerry Lee's version is typically perverse in that the subject of the song shifts from a woman who's so mean that she fucks with an angry face, to ... well, to the Killer himself, who pinches the spotlight in the first verse and never relinquishes it. Oh, the mean woman gets a nod or two, mostly in the form of lascivious ogling of ruby lips and shapely hips, but apparently more urgent for Jerry Lee is a discourse on his love for coffee and tea. As always, the lyrics take a back seat to their filthy delivery, which takes a back seat to Jerry Lee's piano playing, which takes a back seat to nothing and no one. By the end, "Mean Woman Blues" is the Killer's only (with help from the rock-steady trio of Roland Janes, J.W. Brown, and Jimmy Van Eaton, of course). And it's become the standard bearer: when Roy Orbison released his version of the song in 1963, he assaulted welcoming charts with Jerry Lee's arrangement, substituting his own name for Jerry Lee's in a kind of a geeky, understudy eagerness that somehow works.

Seated onstage, he cocks his head, looks over his right shoulder at the smoke-filled crowd, lets a rolled "l" escape from juvee hall and issues a grand "onyourmarksgetsetgo" glissando that leads to a suspenseful "Mmmm" before the flag is dropped: "I got a woman, mean as she can be!" Barrie Jenkins, on cue from the cheers of recognition erupting before the first line is out, sprints out of the gate with a snare roll, and the 40-minute gallop is on. What follows sets the benchmark for the rest of the album: loud, crashing, and impossibly fast.

"Mean Woman Blues" smokes. Pete Harris' bass is warmly recorded, providing ample road for Jerry Lee's jalopy-joyride of a performance, and Jenkins and John Allen ably keep up, Jenkins punishing his ride cymbal in double-time and Allen battening down the hatches with a clipped rhythm, tossing out tentative licks at the ends of some lines — but for all intents and purposes the Nashville Teens sound astonished, as if they've awoken on a carnival ride at the crest of a steep hill. Jerry Lee's left hand is bedrock: sure, cocky, clock-perfect. His right hand virtually stages a show itself: rooster-like in its swagger, proud, flashy. Thirty seconds into the song and you can feel the sense of wire-taut fun and abandon, and the palpable fear that the whole thing might fall apart soon if the players aren't careful. The Nashville Teens pay close attention to the verses — remember, only 30 seconds before they didn't know what song they were going to be playing — and hit the stops well, though the Killer rushes through them, impatient.

Soon the song arrives at the place everyone in the crowd is waiting for, the first solo — Jerry Lee lets loose a *yeah-hah!* and pistons his right hand in eighth notes while Jenkins and Harris squeeze shut their eyes and go along for the ride, borne aloft by a delirious whistle from the crowd. The glissandos are hysterical now. Jerry Lee tosses Allen his first guitar solo, which he plays well, raw and choppy, though it's hard to hear in the mix and beneath his bandmates' bashing around. Jerry Lee speeds up and barks "Go!" to the band — impatient to get back on mike?

Testing the band's endurance? By the time the Killer does butt back in to holler that he ain't bragging but you know it's understood that when he does something he does it mighty good, it sounds like redundant boasting.

But in case the crowd isn't convinced, he drops things down for a relatively quiet, minute-and-a-half break where he plays some fun with his right hand and gets cute vocally, and the tune loosens up and really starts to swing. And this is where any cultural blockades that there might be between the Killer and his audience crumble, brick by brick. Alan Clayson makes an interesting observation: "Coupled with a time-honoured Teutonic fondness for heavy-handed rhythm, the directness of rock & roll's repetitious lyrics enabled those adults who couldn't comprehend a word of English to be swept along emotionally, even become superficially aroused, by 'Hound Dog' more readily than their opposite numbers in the U.K. who dismissed any opus containing 'ain't' as gibberish, a guttersnipe corruption of the language." Robert Palmer was onto it, too: "Rocking out, REALLY ROCKING OUT the way Jerry Lee Lewis did on 'Whole Lotta Shakin' Goin' On' and still does every time he sits down at a piano, is the most profoundly revolutionary statement an artist can make in the rock and roll idiom. It bypasses language, obliterates social conditioning, fulfils a basic human need for rhythmic movement, arouses primal hungers, and suggests how one can go about gratifying them." Palmer adds with a wink, "If you don't believe me, go out and buy a fifth of Jack Daniels, get together with the sexual partner of your choice, and play the record again, real loud."

What language barrier? During the breakdown in "Mean Woman Blues" Jerry Lee's *yeah's, oh's, uh-huh's, ooh's*, growls, and general vocal silliness elicit hoarse and happy cheers from the crowd. No translation necessary, *vielen Dank*, for the universal poetry of rock & roll, bluster, and sex; the Killer's strong hands, his arrogant wide-leg splay at the piano, the countless lagers paraphrase the song just fine. At one point in the show Jerry Lee joins in with the crowd as they chant "Jerry!, Jerry!, Jerry! . . ." It's the only word they really need to understand.

He brings the song back up for a few deafening sprints through the chorus, things miraculously speeding up even more until a merciful, crashing finish, with Jenkins collapsing onto his kit after a couple of mini-glissandos amidst delirious whistles and cheers.

After Jerry Lee magnanimously announces his pleasure at being back at the club, he pounds a single thick cord and launches into "High School Confidential" — the 1958 single released just before the marriage scandal — to cheers of recognition. The Nashville Teens have a few seconds longer this time to figure out the damn tune and key, and come barreling in with gusto, mastering the tricky and exciting held-in-air timing of the song's opening. More insane double-time crash and burn follows, and Jerry Lee's *modus operandi* for the evening becomes pretty clear: pummel each song into submission. John Allen plays a more prominent role here, answering the title line in chunky bar-chords that help fuel the song's zoom and teenage spirit. But Jerry Lee's solos are again sadistic exercises in Who's Boss as he nudges the already hopelessly fast tempo as if he might as well be playing alone; the band simply has to keep up. Luckily the ferocious song is over in a blink; with the exception of professional coupling in certain alleys and establishments, "High

School Confidential" is the fastest two minutes on the Reeperbahn.

The third song on *"Live" At The Star-Club* was actually the third in Jerry Lee's second set. Later, during sequencing in the Philips studio, Loch listened smartly. A slower number, "Money (That's What I Want)" gives both the Nashville Teens and anyone in the crowd who's already sucking wind a bit of a respite. It's also, arguably, the greatest performance on the album. Jerry Lee had recorded the Janie Bradford/Berry Gordy soon-to-be standard in the fall of 1961 for a Sun single, a version hemmed-in by a corny "twist" arrangement, squealing horns, and backing singers faithful to Barrett Strong's 1959 original; vocally, Jerry Lee sounds uncommitted — actually, he sounds embarrassed. But at the Star-Club, the song turns into everything that its champions boast: it's desperate, pleading, funny, rancorous, and utterly confident. It is tempting to think that Jerry Lee is singing about, and to, his depleted bank accounts, relatively barren coffers that at this point in his checkered career he's always hollering on the road in order to fill. But I should resist a facile biographical reading; whatever Jerry Lee's motives, he sings the song with tremendous conviction backed by a band matching him in confidence. The sexiest groove of a long sweaty night, "Money" is a full-band triumph.

I'm imagining that Jerry Lee rubs his fingers together in the widespread sign for moolah before he lays down the opening signature riff; the Nashville Teens drop in behind him — they've been playing this number for years — and propel the song in a lively, muscular way aided by the crowd's hoots and whistles. And Loch's recording — warm, fat, and loud — simply sounds great. A mid-paced groove, "Money" allows Jerry Lee and the band to stretch a bit and interact, Allen's syncopated riffs dodging in and out of Jerry Lee's and Jenkins' playing so that, by the time Jerry Lee starts singing, the tune sounds unstoppable, the 12-bar chassis coasting on grease; throughout, Jenkins powerfully nails down the verses to the floor with his snare and tom (missing once slightly, on the last verse). A few minutes in, Jerry Lee indulges another opportunity to stretch the song a bit, turning the heat down and letting Harris' walking bass lead the way as he riffs on wanting and needing the long green, punctuating his pleas with odd *hah-hah's* and hiccups that break up the crowd; he brings the levels down pretty low (foreshadowing the famed dynamics coming up in "Whole Lotta Shakin' Goin' On") before lifting everything up in the air again with his might and letting it land with a thud on the stage. A brawny performance, and one of the greatest recordings by anyone of that seminal song.

In one of the album's rare audible edits, Loch segues into "Matchbox," another calmer number. Jerry Lee had released a sprightly version of this Carl Perkins tune on his self-titled debut in 1958. At the Star-Club he drawls it in a lazy, countrified way, and the Nashville Teens again step into the arrangement with comfort and poise. The less frantic pace allows for a grinning, showboat solo from Jerry Lee eliciting an excited "Yeah!" from someone close to the audience mike. But what's special about the tune is Allen's guitar solo: raw, sloppy in the best way, and expressive (and audible!).

What Loch has been preparing us for is "What'd I Say," the most combustible and frenzied performance on the album. Three years had passed since the song had given Jerry Lee a rare, if not monster, hit on the *Billboard* singles charts, blessedly rescuing him from the commercial wilderness, and the Killer had great fondness for the tune both as a lucky charm and as a barnstorming, bring-down-the-house live number so in synch with his oversized personality and piano prowess that it seems odd to remember that Ray Charles didn't write the song for him. The long introduction, famous left-hand phrase, and lyrically spare innuendo are ideal for a sexed-up hepcat at a piano. Charles' original 1958 moan-and-sigh recording — born as an onstage improvisation — was ribald enough when Elvis Presley recorded a version and performed it with Ann-Margret in *Viva Las Vegas* in 1963; their dancing duet — kittenish Ann-Margret all black tights and big hair; Elvis studied cool — amplified the sex appeal in the song well within Hollywood and community standards. What Jerry Lee and the Nashville Teens do to the song at the Star-Club could have brought the four of them up on assault charges, even in an area where men freely walked about with handguns. Though Allen's syncopated chords dance nicely with Jerry Lee's, the four-in-the-bar, wall-of-noise pounding isn't relieved by much subtlety, and though it's unlikely that a drummer at his age (19) and with his experience is winded, Jenkins misses some stops, and he and Allen come in a beat late, sloppily, more than once, which only adds to the messy, cantankerous appeal of the song's first part. And Jerry Lee isn't helping much by pushing up against the fast beat mercilessly.

The Killer isn't pleased with what he hears as the band's carelessness. As the song suspends and then tilts toward its second part, Jerry Lee leans back to his band and, off-mike, barks "Play that thing right, boy!" probably to Jenkins, who must be gasping for air. An unfortunate, disciplinarian moment from the Killer caught on tape in perpetuity — and not altogether just either, as he's the one who's keeping the band, whom he treats as hired guns, waiting before each song for the direction toward which they'll have to bound, clutching their instruments, their balls, and their pride in the leap.

Anyway, the band does straighten up. They ignore the tricky stops altogether this time around and the second part of "What I'd Say" is ferocious, highlighted by a break-down where Jerry Lee insanely scats, growls, and goofs his way on top of the Teens' 12-bar groove guided by Allen's lead and made expectant by Jenkins' soft cymbal playing. The thing builds and builds to whoops, whistles, and cheers from the crowd until Jerry Lee ends the cacophony with a final collision on the keys.

Sweaty joy all around.

End of the first side.

Let's head to the back bar.

On the same night that Jerry Lee Lewis is igniting the stage at the Star-Club in Hamburg, John Lennon, Paul McCartney, George Harrison, and Ringo Starr are out and about in London downing scotch-and-cokes, sizing up the competition at a local club. Or maybe they're heading to bed relatively early for men in their early twenties, as they have dialogue to memorize and scenes to film for *A Hard Day's Night* early the next morning, and indeed for much of the week. The boys are more-or-less living in London permanently now, having left Liverpool and the provincial North behind, and in between shooting sequences in faux dressing rooms and police stations and along London's Thames River, they will write songs, rehearse for upcoming one-off shows around town, and gear themselves for their first concerted international summer tour. And all the while they will be pinching themselves, because on this week of April 4, 1964, the Beatles will set a record that will likely never be broken, holding all five of the top positions on the *Billboard* Hot 100, their new single "Can't Buy Me Love," released on the day Jerry Lee was paying the Deutschlandhalle, sitting at #1. Such were the extraordinary rumblings coming from England while Jerry Lee was tearing it up on the Reeperbahn.

Meanwhile on this same April evening, another upstart group of long-haired English musicians was banging together noise and kicking up screams: the Rolling Stones were playing two shows at the Gaumont Theatre in Ipswich, on the east coast of England. London's newest recording sensation were 11 days away from the release of their debut album. The Old Guard? Elvis was bored in Hollywood, U.S.A. on April 5, stuck between filming wooden scenes for his latest movie (*Roustabout*) and glumly if gamely recording such Hill-and-Range classics as "Poison Ivy League" and "It's Carnival Time" for a pitiable soundtrack. Chuck Berry, recently granted parole and carefully putting his troubles with the Mann Act behind him, was rewarded by the U.S. Government in April 1964 with an opportunity to tour the U.K. for the first time, an engagement that he would launch to great success the following month. And his recent singles "Nadine" and "No Particular Place To Go" were charting.

Pull back and view a troubling landscape in widescreen: hair's getting longer, skirts are getting shorter. The rumor is that Jerry Lee trimmed his hair after his 1963 tour of England, dismayed with the look of girly locks on young guys, and Nick Tosches imagines him both lovin' and hatin' those miniskirts "that barely covered the source of all sorrow." Harmonies are getting brighter and beat groups are becoming fashionable, and politics and Vietnam and the Pill and "My Generation" and free love and Swingin' London and the Velvet Underground and Dylan and cannabis and LSD and student protests and forced integration are becoming clearer than merely feared apparitions on the fabled horizon. Whither the Killer?

The second half of *"Live" At The Star-Club* barrels past in a blur, seven songs with a blessed breather in the middle. Loch leads off with "Great Balls Of Fire," followed by "Good Golly Miss Molly" and "Lewis Boogie." Jerry Lee cruises comfortably through his early classic single, a lifetime away at this point, done in under two brusque minutes. Jerry Lee had cut Little Richard's "Good Golly Miss Molly" a year and a half earlier as one of his last Sun singles, and at the Star-Club Jenkins bravely adopts original drummer Buddy Harman's galloping snare-rolls through the verses, propelling this version mightily. Allen lays down another wonderfully shoddy solo that is sadly undermixed by Loch (who might have been threatened by the spirit of the dominating Killer when he was bent over the mixing boards).

"Lewis Boogie," a deafening sprint through Jerry Lee's statement of purpose, is begun and finished in a boisterous 90 seconds. The Nashville Teens seem to have come to an understanding at this point, reached backstage, or whispered *sotto voce* in the tour bus, or yelled in firebaptism under stage lights, I don't know: after nearly three weeks with the Killer, the easiest thing to do is bash away in 4/4, have fun walking the bass, get off on the boys and the girls shaking their heads in glee, be mindful of the stops and changes, and make *damn* sure that you end when he does. Jerry Lee doesn't need much more accompaniment than that, and that's not a criticism of him or of the Nashville Teens; onstage at this point in his career, Jerry Lee is a fierce showman who's interested chiefly in reveling in and translating extreme sensation. If you're in his backing band, just take a deep breath and jump in, it'll be over in under an hour.

The album's last three songs are virtually a reverse image of the trio that kicks off the second side. "Hound Dog" and "Long Tall Sally" are breakneck rips through Elvis' and Little Richard's signature tunes, Jerry Lee doing his best to deconstruct the source material and, blowing away the sparks and smoke, build the tunes back up in his image — and he succeeds on sheer nerve and noise. The closer, "Whole Lotta Shakin' Goin' On," begins with the rumbling of Jerry Lee's left hand, soon beefed up by Harris' fat-bottom bass. The Killer pulls out the stops here as he's now accustomed to, is in fact expected to, do: bench goes flying; grand piano groans as he stands and leans his weight on the keys, pounding them into submission; hair springs free; crowd erupts. "Whole Lotta Shakin' Goin' On" both swings *and* stomps, a sonic combination that few musicians can pull off. Allen's rancorous solo this time is mixed up-front and shoves the song in a really nasty direction. During the quieted "Shake, baby, shake" breakdown (another language lesson), Jerry Lee states his sensible Killer Policy: "If you ain't got something by the end you ain't gonna get nothin'. I guarantee ya." It should've been printed in German on the posters.

What Loch slots between those six numbers throws a different kind of light. His voice made poignant by the bourbon, Jerry Lee turns to the crowd, makes sure he's close to the mike: "Gonna slow it down for ya now, we hope you enjoy this one, a pretty good one, a beautiful song, written and recorded I believe in nineteen hundred and fifty-one or nineteen hundred and fifty-two, somethin' like that — but anyway, one entitled 'Your Cheatin' Heart.'" It's the longest sentence that he'll say all night to a half-comprehending crowd of drunks, and he makes sure that he gets it right, underlining the love and respect that he has for Hank Williams and for this classic. Jerry Lee has often cited Williams as one of the few stylists who influenced him, and his tenderness and affection are borne out in this heartfelt and emotionally raw version. What Cub Koda called "the unofficial anthem of country music" gets a powerful honky-tonk reading filtered through bar-band sincerity and is, along with "Money," one of the highlights of *"Live" At The Star-Club*. By 1964, MGM had already released more than 20 Hank Williams compilations of various quality; it's likely that the natives at the Star-Club knew the song well and were swaying to the hillbilly vibe, already getting off on the Hank Myth, maybe even a few crying into their lagers.

What they wouldn't have been very familiar with were Jerry Lee's original studio versions of "Your Cheatin' Heart". He'd cut the song in March of 1958 in the heady days before the marriage scandal, between readying "High School Confidential" for release and tackling dozens of numbers for potential singles and album tracks, again in January of 1960 in the last sessions at 706 Union, and again in September of 1963 during the *The Golden Rock Hits Of Jerry Lee Lewis* recordings for Smash. The Sun versions were among the many tracks that Sam Phillips deemed unworthy for various reasons, and wouldn't find official release until the early 1970s. It was just as well:

Jerry Lee sings over-respectfully on all three versions (though marginally less so on the 1958 take), trying to do the song justice but floundering in unfamiliar territory by overcompensating and pulling back on his persona. The results sound tentative and uncommitted, and aren't helped by noisy band arrangements that pay scant attention to the quietly reproachful, head-hanging feel of Williams' original.

But onstage it falls into place. Maybe Jerry Lee needed to slow the pace again, maybe he needed an audience, the rapport and empathy, even if wholly imagined, of fellow men whose hearts have been torn by corrupt women. (Never mind the hypocrisy.) At the Star-Club he sings "Your Cheatin' Heart" sincerely, as if he's trying to crawl into the words and make some sense of them, opposite the barely understandable wailings in the signature rock & roll hits. The Nashville Teens respond in kind, swinging commandingly through the country changes; Jerry Lee adds right-hand flourishes that mock the pathos of the words; the bridge arrives tight with energy and lift. But the real star is the Killer's vocal — when Jerry Lee refers to himself by name here it's personal, not showy. Hardcore honky-tonk, soft around the frayed edges. Colin Escott describes the performance as a one-man tour de force, "a stunning fusion of everything that was Jerry Lee Lewis. The bluesy piano licks thrown into the middle of a stone hillbilly classic and a vocal of scorching intensity." Wonders Escott, "Could this really be yesterday's man?"

Following his last number, Jerry Lee stands to boisterous applause, wipes his brow, waves, declines an encore, and disappears to the dressing room where he receives wide-eyed well-wishes from the other musicians on the bill, from friends, strangers. Bourbon is opened, poured, and enjoyed. Horst-Dieter Fischer remembers Jerry Lee turning to him and saying, "It's a pity and a handicap that these shows are being recorded for an album because I have to cling to the mike. I can't do a show like I want to. But I hope that the recordings will be better this way."

Bis später, baby.

Three songs were recorded by Loch in addition to the 13 that comprised *"Live" At The Star-Club*. Sadly, the tapes of "You Win Again" and "I'm On Fire" have been lost. Hopefully they'll turn up in someone's bottom drawer. The show's actual opening number, a vigorous, barnstorming "Down The Line," was not included on the album in its initial release — it was held back for a six-song compilation EP out within the year — but has thankfully been appended to recent reissues. Having initially been conceived without Mercury's permission, and released exclusively in Europe, the album itself has suffered the predictable ups and downs in terms of availability. As I write, *"Live" At The Star-Club* is out of print in the United States. Short of calling for a constitutional amendment to correct this astonishing oversight, I will say that it's criminal that the Killer's *best* rock & roll album, and one of the great rock & roll albums by anyone, is not readily available for domestic purchase, having fallen victim to market politics and licensing red-tape.

(Side note: King Size Taylor is adamant that the bulk of *"Live" At The Star-Club* was concocted after April 5 via knobs and faders. "It's common knowledge that most of the Star-Club Live recordings were in fact made in the Polydor Studio in Hamburg, produced by Siggi Loch, my own included." Taylor continues, "only a few real live stage performances were ever recorded, of which the

'64 Jerry Lee Lewis album was one, but due to the lack of proper studio equipment not being on hand in the club, everything was broken down and totally re-mixed." The result? "Not one recording ever created the sound and the atmosphere of the club." Loch vehemently denies this. "I recorded the first single with King Size Taylor and this was done at the Polydor Studio in Hamburg," he says. "He was produced thereafter by somebody else for Ariloa. Since Ariola was trying to follow the success of my earlier live recordings they faked some studio stuff and just called it 'Live at the Star Club'." Insists Loch: "All the Star Club 'live' recordings that I produced were actually recorded at the Star Club stage.")

The album was released in July of 1964 on Philips in Germany — there it performed well on the charts, reaching the ninth spot — and then the following year in England, in both mono and stereo. In 1980 Phonogram (a joint venture between Philips and Deutsche Grammophon) released the album again in the U.K. "In an era when 'live' albums have become commonplace," Colin Phillips observed in the liner notes, "it may be difficult now to imagine the tremendous interest that was aroused when this album ... first appeared in England as a highly sought after import from Germany". The estimable Bear Family reissue label in Germany rescued the album in 1989, adding "Down The Line," and again in 1994. The album (oddly absent "Down The Line") wasn't released in America until 1986 on Mercury, and again on CD in 1992 through the capable, championing hands of Rhino Records. I picked up this CD and it blew me away, and does every time I listen.

Disgracefully common to all *"Live" At The Star-Club* releases for years has been the cover photo: the European versions incorrectly show Jerry Lee and the Nashville Teens in a pic snapped by Loch at the Deustchlandhalle on April 4; the Rhino version features a shot of Jerry Lee backed by his later touring band, culled from the cover of his *Memphis Beat* album from 1966. The Bear Family release remedied this somewhat by using a fantastic, moody photo of the Star-Club exterior on their issue (and accompanying it with some great photos inside). But *"Live" At The Star-Club* deserves its cover to be graced with one of the many photos taken of the stage show that night that captures the great venue and the Killer in their glory.

What of the Nashville Teens? After they recovered from the U.K. and German tour they settled happily back in Surrey and enjoyed the considerable success of "Tobacco Road." Their appearance at the Star-Club was a fruitful one: in addition to the album, they released two Star-Club Records singles and appeared on two Star-Club Records compilations within a year. They enjoyed tours backing Chuck Berry, Carl Perkins, and Bo Diddley, and also played the United States, but back home could never recapture the chart success of their debut single, though they did place three more songs in the U.K. Top 40 over the next several years. Various band permutations and defections followed: in 1966 Harris departed, and later that same year Jenkins left to join the Animals, playing on many of their seminal tracks; John Hawken left in 1968 and formed Renaissance, and later played in Spooky Tooth and the Strawbs. By the late 1960s, though still playing well-received gigs, the Nashville Teens were virtually finished as a working band.

A talented r&b group, which at their peak matched up with the best London bands of the era in skill and passion, the Nashville Teens lacked, critic Bruce Eder laments, "one (or more) interesting personalities in their ranks that could be put before the public and a collective personality that could be defined, musically or any other way. Neither Sharp nor Phillips was as compelling or interesting a singer as, say, Denny Laine of their Decca Records rivals the Moody Blues, much less Mick Jagger, John Lennon, Paul McCartney, Eric Burdon, or Roger Daltrey." Eder adds, "They never had a sound, beyond the crunching attack on 'Tobacco Road,' that could be identified." Today, original singer Ray Phillips, the only member dating to the band's heyday, still on occasion trots out a version of the Nashville Teens for one-off gigs and festivals, riding the seemingly endless Sixties Nostalgia wave.

Kudos. Characteristic of the near-unanimously effusive reactions to *"Live" At The Star-Club* over the years are Milo Miles' rave in *Rolling Stone* — "'Live' At The Star Club, Hamburg* is not an album, it's a crime scene: Jerry Lee Lewis slaughters his rivals in a thirteen-song set that feels like one long convulsion" — and Stephen Thomas Erlewine's on allmusic.com — "Words cannot describe — cannot contain — the performance captured on *'Live' at the Star Club, Hamburg,* an album that contains the very essence of rock & roll." Much testifying abounds. Detractors complain of the album's crashing noisiness, the lack of subtlety with which Jerry Lee revisits the songs, the fact that the piano is mixed too loudly, but what is certain is that Siggi Loch on this spring evening captured something brutally honest about the Killer, about the primal and timeless center of the very best rock & roll, and about what a relic of the previous decade had to say in the face of new signs and messages.

I was first exposed to the song "High School Confidential" on *Over There* from 1982, a live EP recorded by the Blasters, the L.A.-based band that owed quite a debt to the Killer. My friends and I would drink, jam to the song, marvel at the band's ferocious tightness, coolness, and humor embodied in their version. Phil Alvin's timeless vocals do everything necessary to reinvest the overplayed tune with freshness, to blast away the Fifties corn.

To this day, *"Live" At The Star-Club* amazes Phil's brother Dave Alvin, founder of the Blasters and an acclaimed singer-songwriter. "The Star Club record is without a doubt one of the top ten rock & roll records of any era," Alvin says. "Pure passion, mayhem, sweat and trouble. The fact that rock critics don't celebrate this LP has always astounded me. Not to sound arty or bohemian or philosophical, but it's a performance that can only be called 'deconstructivist.' If that's a word. Jerry Lee deconstructs rock & roll in order to save it. On the other hand, it's a deeply spiritual record where you have a ringside seat to Jerry Lee's personal battle between God and the Devil over the fate of his soul."

He adds: "All that and it *rocks* like hell!"

Was Jerry Lee Lewis playing this hard every night in 1964? More evidence was amassed in October, when Smash released a live album recorded in Alabama three months after the Star-Club performance. It's tempting, in a romantic, mythologizing, historically irresponsible way, to imagine that when Jerry Lee returned to the road in the U.S. on April 10, he raised the roofs of venues with the same insanity and authority that he had in Hamburg. Between his arrival back home and the June 1 release of a new single, he wedged in two grueling tours through the

Midwest, playing one-nighters and several colleges and universities. I wonder: at the Concordia Lounge, in his hometown of Ferriday, Louisiana, on April 10, or at the Field House Auditorium at Notre Dame University on May 16, or at the Val-Air Ballroom in Des Moines, Iowa on May 18, did Jerry Lee again reach rock & roll nirvana? In addition to the performance and the recording, the success of *"Live" At The Star-Club* stems from the historic and cultural notoriety of the Reeperbahn, the hindsight-power of the Beatles' ghosts ruling the venue, and the universal idiom of rock & roll translated to a largely German-speaking crowd. These indelible factors were absent in a one-off gig in Nowhere, Oklahoma. Did Jerry Lee rock as hard, as memorably, as urgently?

He spent the remaining months of 1964 with one eye on the courts and the other on the long road.

In late November, he flew to England for another sold-out, three-week tour, his fifth U.K. visit of his career and second of the year. Unable to bring his American touring band because of difficulties with work permits, Jerry Lee was backed by the Plebs, formed by singer Terry Crowe and guitarist Mick Dunford, two ex-members of the Nashville Teens. The Plebs would release one single in their brief career (the b-side, "Babe I'm Gonna Leave You," an r&b number, has on occasion been anthologized) and are otherwise forgotten but for having been the latest in a line of kids forced to wear blindfolds behind the mercurial Killer. The tour rolled toward 17 shows, two radio appearances, a brief movie cameo (*Be My Guest*) and, more notably, another television appearance, this time on *Ready, Steady, Go!*, the wildly popular, youth-edged program that would run for two years neck-and-neck with the exploding rock & roll scene in England. It was broadcast on Friday nights, kicked off excitingly with the phrase every teenager wants to hear — "The weekend starts here!" — and featured full-length performances of songs. A remarkable pop culture product of the era, *Ready, Steady, Go!* has left behind a reminder of the screamingly propulsive mid-1960s atmosphere of Beatles haircuts, go-go boots, and weekly American and British bands, each newer than the last, reinterpreting rock & roll and r&b for a receptive, shifting world.

Like his Granada special from seven months earlier, Jerry Lee's appearance has been saved in perpetuity on video, and we're the luckier for it. His *Ready, Steady, Go!* slot came on the second night of the tour following a warm-up gig at Colston Hall in Bristol. Jerry Lee chose to sing "Hi-Heel Sneakers," a Top 20 hit for Tommy Tucker in 1964 and a number on the lips and hips of a lot of musicians, so catchy and irresistible is the strut and ethos of the simple, 12-bar song. Jerry Lee had been fooling around with it between sets for months. It was also his new single. He was focused on promotion, and what better advertisement could there be than the Killer surrounded again by adoring teens?

Described by host Keith Fordyce in his onstage intro-duction as "one of the all-time greats of rock & roll," Jerry Lee is wearing a snugly tailored, three-button dark grey jacket, a wide-striped white shirt, and dark tie. By the time the camera pans to him he's already bordered on three sides by clapping kids and he's already smirking, smiling and winking at the camera, his sideburns a bit longer on this visit. Within 30 seconds it's clear that Jerry Lee is gonna really sell this one, dropping in double-time flourishes with both hands before the first verse is over, digging the groove, slipping into it easy and early, egging on the Plebs behind him to thump each measure. By the end of the song he's hollering out the words to the dancing teens surrounding him.

He follows with "Whole Lotta Shakin' Goin' On" which elicits the predictable roar and screeches of delight. The Plebs have a great time on this one, the organ snaking in and out of the rumble, an insistent bee to pollen. Jerry Lee's standing up by the second chorus but manages to stay still long enough for the camera to zoom in for an extended close-up of his sweaty face. Then the jacket's off and the Killer's up on the piano and by the end he's yelling and hollering, his hair wild, his hips moving without subtlety into the faces of the bangs- and pageboy-cut girls who are curious and crotch-level.

The song crashes down inevitably — "Whole Lotta Shakin' Goin' On" *always* must end and isn't that the problem? — as Jerry Lee whips his jacket around his head in manic circles and a wide-shot reveals a crowd of kids stomping and cheering and clueless to the *has-been* label that the Killer, with great aplomb, has just flicked off, yet again.

A few moments into "Hi-Heel Sneakers," Jerry Lee hits his first solo and leans back slightly, gazing upward into the bright ceiling lights to brace himself for the pounding, but also, it seems — his eyes distant, a semi-sickly smile glued onto his face — to stare his way through that ceiling toward a once-glimpsed future. That vision blurs a bit with each drink, lurches into focus with each pill, is fantasized again with each single and album, but always slips damningly from his reach. Anyway, this song will help. And it does. It always does. It's got to. In the last calendar year, beneath the din of something new and unimpeachable rocketing past him, Jerry Lee Lewis sincerely reveled in the redemptive power of his songs and in what, in an endless era of surprising and self-made loss, he's found.

DOWN THE LINE

But one cannot weep and mourn forever, and commerce often healeth a sorrowed heart.

—Nick Tosches

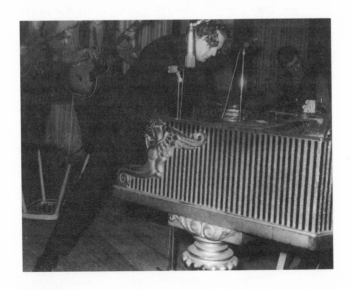

Unrest on the home front. Jerry Lee Lewis' manager Frank Casone had been tangling Jerry Lee's finances in alleged schemes with Sam Phillips involving future Sun Records releases. He'd also locked horns with Jerry Lee's booking agent who was continuing to navigate the maelstrom of long-highway, one-night stands, while Casone was aiming for more lucrative, high-end engagements at larger cities and venues such as Las Vegas. With pride and dog-eared agreements in hand, neither man would budge. Casone eventually took Jerry Lee to court on breach of contract charges, astonishing all concerned with a small-print bombshell that Casone, as per the agreement signed in 1963, was owed a quarter of all show receipts and record royalties and half of any television and film contracts. Casone was smart: sniffing commercial blood, he intuited that Jerry Lee's television profile was about to ascend within the year via appearances on *Shindig!* and other programs. While Jerry Lee was playing, whooping, and whoring it down in Florida, a judge at a court hearing in Memphis decreed that a quarter of all earnings be held in escrow until the courts decided if Jerry Lee had in fact broken his contract as Casone alleged, by not allowing Casone to act as full-time manager.

Meanwhile, Jerry Lee asked "What the hell ya done for me lately?" and vowed to fight. And the endless touring resumed.

In the midst of all of the legal messiness, a new single timidly appeared. "She Was My Baby (He Was My Friend)" backed with "The Hole He Said He'd Dig For Me" wouldn't do much — actually, do anything — to convince radio programmers that Jerry Lee was ready to compete with the Beatles, Peter and Gordon, Billy J. Kramer, or Mary Wells, all of whom were ruling the *Billboard* Top 10 that week. Too bad: "She Was My Baby," recorded during the "I'm On Fire" sessions, was a comic, radio-ready tale of a girlfriend, best buddy, and fave car going missing under the duped nose of the Killer; the flip side, dating to Jerry Lee's first Smash sessions, was a stately slow-waltz by Marion Turner, a cautionary mortality tale sung with sincerity. The country charts ignored the b-side, ironic considering that all of the elements here are in place for the studio resurgence that Jerry Lee would enjoy in four years. As it was, Smash seemed clueless as how to market his records, divided between Hully-Gullying him for the Beat Combo crowd and indulging his conservative classicist leanings for the country crowd. In the middle he fumed, looking both ways toward promises made and broken.

When Shelby Singleton listened to the *"Live" At The Star-Club* import, he might've felt irritation at his across-pond cohorts for cutting such an astonishing album without Smash's affiliation, or he might've admitted that he dropped the ball. Either way, after the tinnitus in his ears faded, he moved swiftly (and, as a wry Colin Escott put it, surprisingly logically). Smash would release two official Jerry Lee Lewis live albums, *The Greatest Live Show On Earth* in 1964 and *By Request: More Of The Greatest Live Show On Earth* in 1966. Both were destined to suffer in comparison to Loch's recording.

Three short months after visiting Hamburg, Jerry Lee was again surrounded by mikes and recording gear onstage. On July 1 he sat in his native element behind an upright piano for three shows — at 2, 6, and 9 p.m. — in front of 18,000 fans at the Municipal Auditorium in Birmingham, Alabama (according to Singleton, tracks were recorded at Montgomery also). Backing him was his new touring band, the soon-to-be-named Memphis Beats: James Albert "Buck" Hutcheson on guitar, Herman "Hawk" Hawkins on bass, Morris "Tarp" Tarrant on drums, and Larry Nichols on organ, a crack team of drinking buddies and seasoned musicians who had been barreling around the country with Jerry Lee for weeks, white-hot by the time July rolled around. Singleton and Jerry Kennedy prepared for the recording carefully, sensitive to capturing both the Killer who rocked and the Killer who could finesse radio-friendly hooks and arrangements. "Shelby had microphones set up all across the stage," Jerry Lee remembered of the recording. "It was the first time anyone had set up a live recording like that. We really got some momentum goin' out there and it all had to be captured in one take. No second chances. I think Shelby edited out some of the talking, but that was all." Marveling at the wattage in his newest backing band, Jerry Lee said, "That's all we need. We were on the runway. We were revving up and we were ready to take off! . . . We was all the same way. Totally electric."

Except that the voltage dipped somewhere between the performances and the recording. The album begins and ends with 30-second vamps that buzzily bookend ten songs ranging from rock & roll and r&b to country. Jerry Lee, dressed sharp in a black suit, white shirt, narrow white tie, and white-leather shoes, leads with a trademark "Mmmmm" before launching into Little Richard's "Jenny, Jenny," and 40 minutes later wraps things up in typically exuberant fashion with an extended "Whole Lotta Shakin' Goin' On," half of which was delivered standing up and prowling the stage. The performances in between are generally sturdy and energetic, but the album suffers from uneven, muddy mixing that oddly plays down the piano. The overall sound is murky and damp, greatly diminishing the liveliness that the audience, enthusiastic from the first note, clearly enjoyed.

The Greatest Live Show On Earth has had many sincere fans and apologists over the years; Singleton himself feels that it's the most successful album he recorded with Jerry Lee. "It had a natural feel," the producer says. "Nothing phoney, just raw, rockin' Jerry Lee." I find the album flawed and extraordinarily frustrating. Compared to the simple but electric sound of *"Live" At The Star-Club* — which in hindsight seems to have benefited by the technological limitations placed on Loch and his engineer — *The Greatest Live Show On Earth* is the aural equivalent of a memory. That metaphor doesn't work for you? Listening to the album feels like spying on the show through a Municipal Auditorium window.

Some songs fight their way through the muffled mix. Charlie Rich's "Who Will The Next Fool Be" (on which Jerry Lee ignores the Beatles and names Elvis as his competition) and Buck Owens' "Together Again" are lively bar-band swings played with country effortlessness that clearly strike a deeply Southern chord with the crowd. "Hi-Heel Sneakers" so shined through the murk that it was lifted for a single and, to Jerry Lee's and Smash's relief, performed relatively well. As he would on *Ready, Steady, Go!* four months later, Jerry Lee really leans into this one, and by the second verse the crowd is caught up, clapping (mostly) on the beat, and filling Memorial Auditorium with a stirring and spontaneous — and loud — groove. Smash released the rousing single in mid-September, and it climbed to #91 on the *Billboard* charts before vanishing. *The Greatest Live Show On Earth*, released on the first of

October, was buoyed by continued wide-eyed testimonials about the Killer's live shows, Smash's vigorous promotion, and the latent attention of some trade magazines, and so fared a bit better, rising to #71 on the album charts, 45 notches higher than *The Golden Rock Hits Of Jerry Lee Lewis* had managed a year earlier. Delivered to an exhaling Singleton and Smash was a return on their investment; a salve for their badly bruised instincts. Was this an auspicious indicator?

They'd try again within two years, recording Jerry Lee in Fort Worth, Texas at a venue quite hospitable to roots music, a smart choice. On August 20, 1966 Jerry Lee played two loose and intimate shows for a few thousand fans at Panther Hall, a venue built by Corky and Bill Kuykendall to hold televised national bowling tournaments, but which by 1963 had been remodeled for country & western shows and dances, to smashing regional success. *Cowtown Jamboree*, a famed country music concert show, and a Texas treasure, was televised live from Panther Hall on Saturday nights from 6:30 to 7:30, featuring over the years George Jones, Wanda Jackson, Bob Wills, Charlie Louvin, Porter Wagoner, Buck Owens, Dolly Parton, Johnny Cash, Lefty Frizzell, and others. (Here's a charming slice of mid-Sixties Lone Star culture for you: following *Cowtown Jamboree* on Channel 11 were the *Buck Owens Show*, the *Bill Anderson Show*, *Country Music Carousel*, the *Ernest Tubb Show* and, at 10 p.m., wrestling followed by *Roller Derby* at 11:30.) In 1966, Willie Nelson recorded a live album at the Panther Hall ballroom; Smash felt that Jerry Lee would fit the bill nicely.

On the night that Jerry Lee's album was recorded, the LSD-enhanced Beatles were nine days away from playing their last-ever concert (at Candlestick Park in San

Francisco), and the opposite directions that they and Jerry Lee were traveling in the heady summer of 1966 illuminated the vexed state of his commercial and aesthetic stock. Nothing in nature exists in a vacuum — every work of popular art is forged in part, directly or indirectly, as a response to cultural circumstances — but it might be too easy to read Jerry Lee's 1960s albums in the wider context of history, epochs, and waves. He wasn't opening the trade magazines, blinking through his hangover, and shaking his fists daily at long-haired rock & roll, psychedelia, and the general trippiness of youth culture, but he and, more importantly, Smash were reacting consciously to the trends. This makes the music all the more illuminating on *By Request: More Of The Greatest Live Show On Earth* — released in October, as the Beatles were on their notorious break growing moustaches and conceiving of Sergeant Pepper, the Rolling Stones were freaking out and vibing off of "Have You Seen Your Mother, Baby, Standing In The Shadow?", Grace Slick was performing live for the first time with Jefferson Airplane, and the Byrds were eight miles high. Jerry Lee was in danger of suffering from musical schizophrenia, so divided was he among identities, song styles, choices, and native loves at this point in his career.

That said, *By Request: More Of The Greatest Live Show On Earth*, though thinly recorded and sloppily edited, is a pretty tough country album. It's hardly *Concert At Carnegie Hall With Buck Owens & The Buckaroos* or *Johnny Cash At Folsom Prison*, but in hindsight it was a tentative step toward Jerry Lee's commercial rebirth. The album is made all the more appealing by the tight but elastic Memphis Beats, the receptive crowd, and Jerry Lee's relaxed, talkative manner. (I have no idea what was or wasn't coursing through his blood on this hot Texas night, but he is in a good mood.) Sporting an uncharacteristic goatee — a half-bemused concession to Mod culture — Jerry Lee addresses the audience, sometimes specifically, cracking jokes, barking weirdly, chuckling and yapping up a storm, appealingly calling the crowd his "neighbors." He'd busted a rib onstage a couple months before at a gig in Detroit, requiring him to cancel a week's worth of shows, but he sounds fully healed on this night. The set list mixes country with rock & roll as was the Killer's mid-decade custom, and the colorful country tunes are the standouts, especially a trio on the second side — Hank Williams' "You Win Again," Moon Mullican's "I'll Sail My Ship Alone," and Buck Owens' "Cryin' Time" — that renews and celebrates Jerry Lee's bedrock influences, and looks to the near future. Jerry Lee takes his time respectfully introducing Mullican's number, and that marks the evening's comments in general: the Killer's in an admiring mood. Another good tune is "How's My Ex Treating You." Escott points out that it had been a recent regional hit in Fort Worth, so Jerry Lee was certain to haul out the bar-room tear-jerker, which he himself had recorded for Sun in the summer of 1962. The reception, though less raucous, is on par with the Star-Club greetings: the crowd at Panther Hall is grateful for the number and for Jerry Lee's careful, deferential attention. Their obvious pleasure works its way through the band's performance.

By Request: More Of The Greatest Live Show On Earth sounds like a pretty fun night all around, actually, the cowtown throng happy with Jerry Lee's rock & roll songs as well, though relative to the country numbers they sound a tad generic. (Inexplicably, a rousing version of "Lovin' Up a Storm" was left off of the album.) He hauls out a few Chuck Berry songs plus "Money," but the warhorse "What'd I Say" is the performance that merits attention, Jerry Lee dropping things down in the middle to tell a ribald, if shopworn, story about a sweet young thang in the car with him up on a Louisiana levee. He sounds as if he's making it up along the way, his comic timing adequate at best, but when he heats things up by mimicking the thrills shared by his honey and him and the crowd climbs along for the voyeuristic fun, the song picks up speed and rolls around in some good-natured filth and turns into a crowd-pleasing show-stopper.

The country material, sung with respect blended with eased-back confidence, contributes strongly to a strong if uneven album. Jerry Lee would wait a couple years to commit more fully to "the country and western field of music." He returned on November 26 to play Panther Hall and appear on *Cowtown Jamboree* to what I can only imagine was a warm and obliging reception.

In between the release of the two live albums, Smash issued three studio records — *The Return Of Rock* and *Country Songs For City Folks* in 1965, and *Memphis Beat* in 1966 — and a handful of singles. All failed on the charts as the decade mercilessly roared past Jerry Lee Lewis, threatening to erase him completely but for the dust kicked up at his shows. Until the end of the decade, when old-fashioned rock & roll would become (somewhat) cool again in the form of roots revival festivals and charting bands like Credence Clearwater Revival, Jerry Lee couldn't possibly compete with commercial rock & roll radio as he had in the late 1950s.

Television was helping to keep him visible: between the fall of 1964 and the spring of 1966 he would make multiple appearances on *American Bandstand*, *Hollywood A Go-Go*, *The Lloyd Thaxton Show*, *Shindig!*, *The Soupy Sales Show*, *The Clay Cole Show*, and a couple of local programs, *Upbeat* in Cleveland and *Cowtown Jamboree*, hocking his latest singles and breathing vigor into his classics. In between gigs and recording sessions he was either on the road or, ever more sporadically, in the studio. Later, Myra acknowledged that she and her husband spent very few nights together alone during their vexed marriage, as she was either solo for weeks on end or, dubiously blessed with the presence of a pseudo-husband at home, plugging her ears against the early-hours din made by Jerry Lee and his drunk, pill-popping entourage.

Though some fans are likely to disagree, *The Return Of Rock* and *Memphis Beat* sound to my ears like virtually the same album in different finery — further attempts by Smash to package Jerry Lee as a hardcore rock-and-roller who can still compete with the new long-haired sounds. As is usually the case when someone, some philosophy, or some studio ideology tries to control or otherwise steer the Killer, the end result sounds contrived. Each album has its moments, but *The Return Of Rock* is nearly done in before the needle drops by an atrocious cover: decked out in a mummified paisley tux and frilly shirt, smiling wanly, Jerry Lee looks like Liberace's sickly younger brother, while a few teenagers behind him dance in mild bewilderment as if they'd been teleported from the set of *Shindig!* It's a queasy scene, man. But a listen to the album reveals some rockin' moments: Chuck Berry's "Maybeline" features a ripping piano solo, the closest the album will come to marrying boogie-woogie to guitar-based rock & roll, and Hank Ballard's "Sexy Ways," which Jerry Lee had tried to record at Sun in a tamer version, is a pretty filthy grind that takes a lot of risks lyrically and gets away with it. Whenever Jerry Lee gets to slide under a number as sexy and dirty as this, he has a lot of fun. "Baby, Hold Me Close" is a cool studio-concocted groove that sounds as if Jerry Lee and Shelby Singleton were listening to the Blendells' great r&b/garage single "La La La La La" from the previous year; Jerry Lee's tune is essentially a rewrite, but the changes and 12-bar chassis were familiar enough anyway, and he gets his persona around the number.

But "I Believe In You," "Don't Let Go," "Roll Over Beethoven," "Corrine Corrina," and "Johnny B. Goode" each suffers from a predictable arrangement, safe playing from the crack team of session players, and a general sense of unease and desperation, the distressing sound of catching up. Lamely titled, *The Return Of Rock* was released on June 5, 1965 as Barbra Streisand, Herman's Hermits, the Supremes, and Herb Alpert and the Tijuana Brass were chumming it up on the *Billboard* pop album charts. The bespangled commercial ceiling was dropping fast.

Tacking slightly south a year later, Smash repackaged Jerry Lee as a Ferriday hepcat lite on *Memphis Beat*. More than half of the songs were recorded in a two-day blast on January 5 and 6, 1966 at Phillips Studio in Memphis where Jerry Lee was reunited with Sun producer Jack Clement; the other tracks were culled from a rare New York City session eight months earlier and from his first Smash recordings in 1963 (a bottomless haul that would continue to be mined in the future). Again supported by sympathetic if conservative session players, Jerry Lee runs through generally lackluster r&b numbers, Ray Charles refitted with a worrisome eye on the charts. The title track, an attempt to write a signature Killer tune, betrays its self-consciousness in a wordy lyric that tries to do too much and ends up sounding lifted from a Tennessee Department of Tourist Development pamphlet. "Hallelujah, I Love Her So" and "Just Because" light up well, especially the latter, another fine, rollicking example of a song stamped with the Killer's permission to exist. Both recordings dated to the September 1963 sessions, suggesting that Jerry Lee was much happier barreling his way through songs other than the ones he'd already nailed.

Generally, Jerry Lee sounds game here, but "Drinkin' Wine Spo-Dee-O-Dee" (a longtime favorite of his), "Sticks and Stones," "The Urge," and "Big Boss Man" (likely an attempt to revive the stomping piano riff of "Hi-Heel Sneakers") again suffer from a broad and compulsory feel, and by-the-numbers arrangements. "Too Young" is a real laugher, a misguided attempt to see if anyone would buy Jerry Lee in the piano lounge over tinkling martini glasses and evening gowns; his performance is hysterically uncomfortable. Many commentators have cited "Lincoln Limousine" as the strangest track of the bunch: Jerry Lee's oddly toned "tribute" to John F. Kennedy is simply weird, so ambiguous and amateurishly written that it's imposs-ible to determine exactly what motivated him to write it. Any sparks produced between sincere eulogy and deep Southern mistrust of the Northeastern Establishment might have become combustible, but hiding behind Jerry Lee's inability to commit, they're smothered. It is one of the most peculiar songs he's cut in his career. Three strong numbers were recorded around this time: "Skid Row," an unheralded country song dramatizing life's seamier side; Merle Haggard's great "Swinging Doors"; and a fun and rocking original, "This Must Be The Place" (which I first discovered in the Nineties courtesy of a blistering version by the Swingin' Neckbreakers). The latter was tacked onto the flip side of a single, while the first two remained temporarily in the vaults.

I'm not exactly sure what recording masters the Smash publicist was listening to when he carefully wrote on the back of the album, "There's a lot of rock in the Memphis Beat, but experts also see in it the lively vitality of the old riverboat shuffle and that mixture of joy and the blues that is called gospel." Sweating at his copy desk, he adds, "It is a blending of the hot sounds of New Orleans with the soulful echo of spirituals." In theory. Released on May 14, 1966, *Memphis Beat*, despite solid promotion and decent reviews, was again brusquely elbowed out of the way by the likes of the Rolling Stones, the Mamas & the Pappas, the Monkees, the Supremes, and the unsinkable Herb Alpert. And how can we forget *The Sound Of Music* and Staff Sergeant Barry Sandler?

Of greater interest historically, if not artistically, was *Country Songs For City Folks*, released in October of 1965. A product of the stylistic whiplash in Smash's selections of this era, the album nonetheless was, until the end of the decade, the most cohesive album besides *"Live" At The Star-Club* that Jerry Lee would record.

Made over the course of the year in three sessions while Jerry Lee climbed in and out of beds, planes, and tour buses, *Country Songs For City Folks* was an attempt to sell Jerry Lee-styled country to the masses. In the years before *Hee Haw* and artists like Johnny Cash and Kris Kristofferson would help country go mainstream, this was a somewhat dicey proposition. Crossover singles weren't uncommon, but urban audiences wouldn't fully and consistently embrace country music for many more years. But the rumblings were there. The year 1965 has been described as "The Big Country Boom," Bob Millard citing crossover hits by Tex Ritter, Connie B. Gay, and Wesley Rose increasing country music radio coverage in large cities like New York and Chicago, and a spike in overseas and USO shows. Millard also notes that Jimmy Dean's ABC television show was successful, with many syndicated shows springing up in its wake, and "country artists became popular with variety and talk show hosts from Johnny Carson to Lloyd Thaxton, and appeared on such pop shows as *Shindig!* and *Hootenanny.*" Of course, in August Ringo Starr would croon Buck Owens' "Act Naturally" on the Beatles' *Help!* soundtrack album, ensuring that millions would hear the Bakersfield sound (as filtered through Liverpool, anyway).

Smash was casting for ideas on how to move Jerry Lee's music and, sensing this nascent mainstreaming of country, and peering into the man's inexhaustible storehouse of song and inspiration, decided on an album of country songs. Kennedy later lamented to Escott that what derailed the album was a lack of original tunes, as Jerry Lee's iffy chart life had had the predictable consequence of few songwriters knocking on his door. Thus the record makers had a choice: plumb the depths of hillbilly history, or scan the recent country charts for suitable songs. They chose the latter, an approach that might have infused the album with a bold contemporary feel, but unfortunately underscored the crass "covers" feel to the enterprise. As it is, *Country Songs For City Folks* is perhaps best remembered among music historians as the album on which a young Welshman named Tom Jones heard "Green, Green Grass Of Home," inspiring him to record his own version, which would become a giant mid-decade hit, leaving Jerry Lee behind in an all-too-familiar wake.

It seems to me that where Smash dropped the ball was in choosing not to commit to a conceptual framework. So-called "concept albums" hardly began with the Who's *Tommy*; there was a precedent in country music for LPs that told stories in a narrative arc, a borrowing from literature's oral tradition that was native and comfortable in the South. Marty Robbins' *Gunfighter Ballads And Trail Songs* was released in 1959, and Johnny Cash would issue *Ride This Train* (1960), *Blood, Sweat, and Tears* (1962), and *Bitter Tears (Ballads Of The American Indian)* (1964), a trio of Americana albums with thematic underpinnings. Among later story-albums that would garner attention were Porter Wagoner's two 1967 releases, *Soul Of A Convict & Other Great Prison Songs* and *The Cold Hard Facts Of Life*; the latter wasn't explicitly conceptual, but the infamous photo on the jacket made clear the songs' collective theme of marital/romantic regrets and messiness. How interesting it might have been had Smash shrugged off commercial anxiety and built *Country Songs For City Folks* around mid-century rural diaspora, nostalgia, and small-town values tested in large-city ways, and let Jerry Lee — who rarely recorded out of Tennessee but who'd seen the world and its charms and dangers — find his way among the songs.

Country Songs For City Folks is instead a straightforward album of recent charting songs with no discernible lyrical theme. The cover photograph is curious, and telling: Jerry Lee leans against a tree, sky and leaves behind, the image overlaid onto a shot of a brutally utilitarian, modern building, its anonymous, lifeless windows contrasting with the beaming warmth in Jerry Lee's face. (The Philips issue of the album featured a different, no less confused cover: a shot of Jerry Lee from the Deutschlandhalle show

sandwiched between a young woman standing triumphant in a cow pasture and another woman dressed in
contemporary jet age posing confidently in a sleek airport
terminal — enough ham-handed conceptual editing to
cause headaches.) Andrew McRae, who later compiled a
CD reissue of *Country Songs For City Folks*, notes that "The
sparkling windows of a city apartment block were clearly
at odds with the usual rhinestones and wagon wheels that
invariably adorned the covers of Country & Western LPs
of the period. Who was supposed to buy this album? The
city clickers or the Hayride crowd?" Answers McRae, "In
the event it appears that neither camp was satisfied."

The album begins with a warm version of Claude
Putnam's "Green, Green Grass Of Home," a song which
has become a standard down the years but in 1965 was
a fresh hit by Porter Wagoner. Jerry Lee is committed to
the tune — as well as to the echo-laden, jail-cell spoken
middle — and it was one of the more ambitious and
sincerely sung performances he'd release in the Sixties;
the countrypolitan strings and female singers threaten to
over-sweeten the proceedings, but it's a difficult song to
damage, so timeworn and classic is the tear-jerking play
between nostalgia and bitter truth, innocence and guilt.
(Smash wisely released it as a single in October of 1965,
but it stiffed, impudently awaiting Jones' and Bobby Bare's
versions for commercial ascension.) Jerry Lee finds lived-
in places in a few other tracks on the album, such as Hank
Thompson's "The Wild Side Of Life" and, most notably,
"Detroit City," made famous by Bare. A blue-collar lament
written by Danny Dill and Mel Tillis, "Detroit City" is the
kind of bar-room sing-along expressly made to warble
sadly by anyone so far from home that he feels scared,
helpless, and a bit bitter. Kennedy's stinging guitar and the

song's head-hanging shuffle mimic the singer's dilemma, the kind of urban-versus-rural complication that the album could've rallied around.

But the lesser tracks reflect Smash's conservatism: innocuous folk-pop like "Walk Right In" and "King Of The Road" sit next to superfluous versions of "Ring Of Fire" and "Crazy Arms" (Jerry Lee's third version of his debut single). There are some attempts at levity: younger sister Linda Gail (who'd become a highly visible cohort in several years) contributes an ace hillbilly twang to the Gold Rush-saga "North To Alaska," and Jerry Lee has fun with Claude King's "Wolverton Mountain." But in general, *Country Songs For City Folks* suffers from an unhazardous approach that nestles in the merely harmless — hardly a word that one uttered eight years earlier when considering the Killer, and an odious adjective that Jerry Lee had exploded with grinning aplomb in Hamburg. Here, he cannot — or will not — find enough purchase in a musical idiom that he cares enough for to posses and make his own. McRae: "One is only left to imagine Jerry Lee cutting loose on such material and giving us real 'Lewis' versions of these classics, in the way he had dealt with other people's hits in his unfettered days at Sun. Sam Phillips would just let the tapes roll and let Jerry do pretty much what he wanted. Here, however, Shelby Singleton is playing it by the book."

Billboard yawned at *Country Songs For City Folks*, facing as it did the usual long-haired, frosty-lipsticked enemies on the pop album charts. When four years later the album was repackaged as *All Country* following Jerry Lee's rise as a country star, it peaked at #39 on the country album charts, an indication of the unforgiving cracks into which Jerry Lee Lewis regularly fell in the mid-1960s.

There wasn't much left to do but drink, gig, and fuck. Following the release of *By Request* in October of 1966, Jerry Lee resumed his punishing road schedule aided and abetted by drink and pills, rocked Europe hard again, grew a beard, and got serious out in Hollywood playing Iago in *Catch My Soul*, producer Jack Wood's six-week stage revival of *Othello*.

He was unaware that a major turnaround was looming. In March of 1967, Shelby Singleton left Mercury Records to start his own label (where he'd soon score an enormous crossover hit with Jeannie C. Riley's "Harper Valley PTA"). Jerry Lee now became Jerry Kennedy's full-time problem. He had a year and a half left on his contract, and Kennedy had to continue to produce singles and albums for a malevolent pop market, all the while scratching his head over *what the heck to do*. Jerry Lee's lone album in 1967, the curious (and among Killer fans somewhat infamous) *Soul My Way*, was a hodgepodge of old tracks and new that Kennedy attempted to unify with variety show pizzazz. What a strange record it is, all the more notorious for being, as I write, the only 1960s Jerry Lee Lewis album yet to be reissued, continuing to languish in the pricey collectibles market, dim awareness of it made possible by a few stray tracks and low-resolution jpegs of the album cover posted online.

Three tracks ("Wedding Bells," "He Took It Like A Man," "Betcha Gonna Like It") date to the 1963/64 period, and the remaining eight were briskly recorded in two single-day sessions in May and August of 1967. The results are certainly odd, but Kennedy can't be faulted for lack of ambition. An r&b vibe predominates: the opener, Bobby "Blue" Bland's "Turn On Your Love Light," is rousing and horn-driven, far from anything Jerry Lee had ever seriously courted, and if it summons the awkward image of the Killer standing in a spotlight, swinging his mike *à la* Tom Jones, at least it was different; "It's A Hang Up, Baby" followed in style, a 12-bar groove aided by a slick arrangement with nary a piano in sight; Roy Head's venerable "Treat Her Right" and "Betcha Gonna Like It" also worked well in the finger-popping mode. But the album sags in places: "Just Dropped In (To See What Condition My Condition Was In)" is, in hindsight, the predictable nod to fashionable psychedelia, poorly sold by a bewildered Jerry Lee (Kenny Rogers would later make it a hit); Roy Orbison's "Dream Baby" was wimpy and pointless, "Shotgun Man" sadly generic. Shelby Singleton admits, "Jerry Lee just didn't feel the songs."

Despite the up-beat tunes and good-hearted attempt to urbanize the Killer in a commercial-sounding, big band setting, *Soul My Way*, released on November 1, 1967, found no takers on radio and stubbornly refused to chart on *Billboard*, likely a mercy move on the part of an embarrassed record so ignorant of contemporary musical styles and moods that it may as well have been a comedy album: "Please welcome: The Woefully Out-of-Touch . . ."

I don't pretend to know or to fully understand him. He wouldn't speak to me for this book. I leave analysis in the hands of more capable people. What I do know is that in the late 1960s Jerry Lee Lewis started recording songs that were deeply felt. After 1967, he sang sincerely more often than he had before, and we're given a revealing and genuine glimpse of his life through the best songs in that period. Little in his 1960s output approaches the authenticity of his performance on *"Live" At The Star-Club*, as do the recordings begun in January of 1968.

Though hardly destitute, Jerry Lee wasn't rolling in long green as 1967 drew to a close. The *Catch My Soul* gig in the coming months would raise his profile nationally and would pay well, but it was impossible for him to get off the long road for very long if he wanted to keep his toys, his cars, his Golden Eagle tour bus, his friends, and his band. Touring was still a source of fun and pleasure, and he loved playing to appreciative crowds. "I like working," he told an English journalist at the time, "I like to be singing in a club with the people right there, next to me." But shows were often sparsely attended, and old demons metamorphosed as new evils. The giddy blur of boozing and pill-dropping was courted longer and becoming harder to blink out of — he'd later tell Robert Palmer that he'd have to drink a fifth of tequila to sober up and do his shows — and the pussy-chasing in hotels and the confounding violence at home were damaging to 23-year-old Myra.

As a string of brightly lit promises made and delivered, the road bore public and private anguishes for Jerry Lee. He brought most, if not all, of them on himself as he wrestled with selfishness, ego, guilt, and redemption. That noisy, warring horde would soon find a native home in song. In the first week of 1968, an epochal year marked worldwide by violent and permanent repudiation of the establishment by students, protesters, and agitators of all stripes, Jerry Lee Lewis began recording songs in Nashville that couldn't have been more conservative and classicist in form, songs that would forever change his fortunes.

Popular country music is in large part defined by its allegiance to form and standards. There's safety and great comfort to be found in such loyalty. My first brush with country music left me feeling somewhat exposed, having been raised in a home where Nashville songs were scarce, where any pastoral gesture beyond carrying a *Hee Haw* lunchbox was an affectation. Sometime during my early teens I gravitated toward popular country music: in between pulling up my F.M./classic rock roots and brush-cutting a path through New Wave/punk and indie, it seemed a good enough a time as any to scan.

Blaring occasionally on our black-and-white kitchen television while I was growing up, *Hee Haw* had something to do with it, as did Jerry Reed's picking in *Smokey And The Bandit*, and the general CB/trucker mania. So did *Urban Cowboy*, the 1980 movie starring John Travolta and Debra Winger produced expressly to cash in on the country music craze made popular by Mickey Gilley (Jerry Lee's cousin) and his enormous self-named honky-tonk in Pasadena, Texas. Like many trends, the city cowboy craze was prefaced, if not created, by mainstream media machination — in this case a widely read article in *Esquire* magazine, "The Ballad of the Urban Cowboy" in the September 1978 issue — and was short-lived, petering out by 1982 or so. I didn't see the movie at the time and scoffed with my high school buddies at Travolta's earnest cowboy-hat posturing, the mechanical bulls, the sudden cultural infatuation with honky-tonks and corny dancing. But there was something in the air that was lively and interesting, that felt warmly familiar. I started to look around, though I hardly led with intellectual curiosity. The dizzying sight of Tanya Tucker in a black leather body-suit on her *T.N.T.* album, Catherine Bach's endless legs on the *Dukes of Hazzard*, and the denim cutoffs worn by the rope-swinging girls in the Mountain Dew commercials had plenty to do with my sudden interest in all things "rural."

But there was something in the music, too. Many of the artists featured on the *Urban Cowboy* soundtrack weren't pure country artists by any stretch — think Linda Rondstadt, Anne Murray, Jimmy Buffet, the Eagles — but the album sold over a million copies, and Johnny Lee's "Lookin' For Love (In All The Wrong Places)" was inescapable. Country music sales doubled in 1981, reaching a staggering $500 million. Country music was suddenly on pop radio, Lone Star beer bottles clinking together as the money piled up, as Gilley's packed 'em in while Hollywood looked on with interest, and as two-steps and hoe-downs eclipsed the Hustle and the Bump as the latest suburban weekend dance contests. ("I think country music owes John Travolta a huge debt of thanks," Charlie Daniels would later opine.) What the *Urban Cowboy* artists made palpable in their hybrid approach was the timeless formal elements of country music, the lived-in reassurances of lyrical themes and musical tropes. Awash in my puzzling and often frustrating teens, I took odd but great consolation in the predictability of country music.

So one day I opened the *Washington Post*, scanned the local radio listings, and found WMZQ, which I'd listen to at night in my bedroom with the door closed, tuning in to and digging the traditions and the meanings of Nashville-produced popular music, reveling in the formulae, if a bit shyly. I don't know that I was able to tell many aesthetic differences among Barbara Mandrell and Alabama and George Jones and Ronnie Milsap, and the history was certainly beyond me. (Plus, I was getting some of the performers confused with Lynyrd Skynyrd and the Charlie Daniels Band, whose albums my buddies were wearing out.) But I could hear a difference in country music that I wasn't hearing in, say, the Police or, a bit later, in the Dead

Kennedys: a pleasing innocence, an unaffected kindness for the listener, an embrace of corny values that felt so old that they might've been biblical. Though this phase didn't last long — Nashville ended up boring me with its slickness, and I had skinny ties to wear and Mod bulls-eye buttons to pin on my jean jacket — I had developed an affection and appreciation for the promises that country music made and delivered.

That admiration expanded when I discovered Elvis Presley, Sam Phillips, and Sun Records. After college, I moved to Athens in southeast Ohio. Within days of settling in to the blighted west end in a rundown house that looked like it could have been pushed over by hand, I began soaking up the mountain town's old-time hillbilly, bluegrass, and rootsy vibes. I was fairly drenched in alcohol my first few years there (though, miraculously, I managed to get my work done in graduate school) and countless shots of Wild Turkey, a healthy dose of William Faulkner, and the Appalachian honeysuckle breezes stirred up in me a sense of timelessness. Having emerged in Athens County from the Washington, D.C. suburbs, I got off on the looming, shadowy hollers and hills and the far-nearness of the Ohio River, embracing a kind of bedrock Americana. I wasn't then aware of the history of hardscrabble ballads having been imported into Appalachia 200 years earlier by English settlers, but I was cutting through the fading mist of that history. I'd wander past the Blue Eagle music store where Lost John Hutchison, local country-blues and folk legend, would be holding forth and spinning yarns, and I'd hear bluegrass bands at O'Hooleys, where friendly townies would drink and talk with me about Merle Haggard and the Everly Brothers.

My copy of an Elvis double-album compilation (one

of those ubiquitous, inexpensive jobs advertised on TV that I ordered on impulse late one night) arrived just in time. Staggering home after last call at the Union Bar, I'd open my bedroom windows to let in the breeze, play some exhilarating Elvis circa 1954/55 — "Good Rockin' Tonight," "That's All Right," "Trying To Get To You" — and marvel at the ageless Sun echo bouncing around and repeating in the sweetened dark outside. I'd known Elvis, of course. My family had the RCA compilations and I grew up with them and loved them, but I hadn't listened much to his Sun recordings until I moved to southeast Ohio and bought that record, which led me to other Sun artists, which led me to the country and blues artists whom they were covering. It was a heady year moving from Elvis to Carl Perkins to Johnny Cash to Bill Monroe to Hank Williams to Charlie Rich and back again. My education in country music had truly begun, as had an understanding of country's classic and enduring appeal, and its assurances to home and wellbeing.

Two decades earlier, the Killer was listening to those same pledges. It was the Summer of Love and he figured, *what the fuck*. He'd remembered the fond applause in Fort Worth, could never forget that the country audience had bought some of his records during the Fall. And he worshipped Hank and Jimmie. "Country music is three chords and the truth," Harlan Howard famously said. *I can do that*, Jerry Lee thought. *Hell, I live that.*

Between 1963 and 1965 Mercury had 51 artists on their roster in Nashville, and Jerry Kennedy produced or played on the majority of their records. What determined a "successful" artist in the label's view? "Sales," Kennedy answers flatly. "That's what I was programmed for. No matter how it affected a certain number of folks out there, I didn't pay any attention to that. It was always the sales, that was the bottom line." In these terms Jerry Lee had been a monumental failure at Mercury, and he was likely going to be dropped if one or two more tries didn't hit paydirt. "I went to an A&R meeting in Chicago," Kennedy recalls, "and they said, *What else can we do with this guy?*" Maybe the planets were in a line, maybe God took some pity on a damned sinner. Kennedy, a hockey fan, used to travel to Knoxville, Tennessee whenever the Nashville Dixie Fliers were playing the Knoxville Knights. There at the arena he was used to running into Bobby Denton, program director at Knoxville's country radio station WIVK. For a couple of years during these games, Denton, lamenting Jerry Lee's commercial failures, had been bugging Kennedy to cut some stone country records with Jerry Lee. For his part Kennedy, who by 1968 had been hanging with Jerry Lee in the studio for half a decade, didn't necessarily feel that country was the native place to go. "But I was hopin'," he says.

Kennedy considered Denton's enthusiasm and his sharp industry ears and, with Mercury promotional man Eddie Kilroy, approached Jerry Lee at the end of 1967, pitching the idea of recording some songs in Nashville to capture the country audience, the pop charts be damned. Jerry Lee was easy to convince, although, as a man in whom *contradiction* is the active ingredient, he would always have a boot planted firmly on rock & roll soil. "The material I cut for Mercury suited me at the time," Jerry Lee wrote in his autobiography. "It was a way to get in through the back door, to get the disc jockeys to play my records again. I went through the country field, though to me I was still a rock 'n' roller. I was just taking their material and doing it because I knew they were first-class songs. That's the way I did them. I delivered them in my own way. I lived a lot of those songs. As the years go by you get into it — you've lived it. People from all over the world have told me my records have raised their spirits, inspired them, helped make life easier for them — and they've done the same thing for me."

He added, "I listen to other peoples' records all over the world, have done all my life. But I would rather listen to Jerry Lee Lewis records. Not because they are my own records, but 'cause I hear more meaning to it, the deliverance of the vocal or something in the words. It's more substantial. The piano playing and the singing go together and it all speaks to me."

Kennedy's first step was to get the Killer some top-shelf material. "All of the publishers and writers in town were Jerry Lee Lewis fans," Kennedy says. "So that was an easy procurement. I just put the word out and I got the best songs people had. And it stayed like that for years and years." On January 5, Jerry Lee entered Columbia Studio in Nashville with Kennedy, Kilroy, and a group of seasoned musicians, including a young fiddle player and guitarist named Ken Lovelace whom Jerry Lee had met in Louisiana the previous May, and who would stay with him for four decades. Jerry Lee had been off the road for a month and fighting with Myra, and because the *Catch My Soul* rehearsals were scheduled to start in a couple of weeks in foreign and far-away Hollywood, he was itching to play. They cut three tracks on that chilly Friday afternoon, the Ernest Tubb classic "Walking The Floor Over You" and two new originals secured by Smash, "All The Good Is Gone" and "Another Place, Another Time."

The latter, a last-call lament written by Jerry Chestnut,

was the song that gave Jerry Lee a new vocabulary of legitimacy, and an entrée into the world of unadulterated honky-tonk. A classic mid-tempo weeper, the song's accompaniment is understated but crucial, and mixed beautifully: the snare doesn't crack too loudly; the fiddle mourns without affectation; the female backing singers complement the sorrow without treacle. But the key to the tune's success is the vocal, assured and confident — no surprise there — but wounded at the vulnerable center, a kind of pathos no one had heard coming from the Killer in years. Nick Tosches describes a "beautiful song of anguish and loneliness": Jerry Lee sings "with the voice of one trying to conceal rather than reveal that anguish and that loneliness." Tosches adds, "When Eddie Kilroy and the musicians who were in the studio that day heard that voice, they felt shivers like cold crawling things up and down their spines, and they closed and opened their eyes, breathing, as if to shake loose a sudden inward fright." The Jerry Lee who sings "Another Time, Another Place" sounded fresh, remade, genuine; it was his purest reading of country blues since "Your Cheatin' Heart" at the Star-Club four years earlier. Everyone in Columbia that day knew that they had something.

A single was scheduled for release in February; further recording sessions were scheduled for April. In between, Jerry Lee gamely moved Myra and extended family out to sunny California in an apartment off Sunset Boulevard, where they lived for three months. Myra soaked up the new domestic arrangement, however cobbled together, and enjoyed driving down the palm-tree thoroughfares wide-eyed in the presence of celebrities and their palatial homes. Jerry Lee winced in the sunlight and threw himself into contemporary Shakespeare and the character of Iago, likely luxuriating in the soldier's treachery and meanness. (Jack Good had convinced Jerry Lee to play Iago by assuring Jerry Lee that he was born to the role. "You're the only one I know as evil as he is," Good reportedly said to the Killer.) He got to play a few numbers at the piano, barking Iago's schemes and desires in Ferriday boogie-woogie and blues on songs like "Let a Soldier Drink" and "Lust of the Blood," and his Southern-accented readings of his lines were oddly effective. Critics from *Variety* to *Newsweek* enjoyed the show and reviewed it positively. *Catch My Soul* played for six weeks at the Ahmanson Theater in Los Angeles to consistently full houses and to the welcome sound of raining coin.

There was some talk of the show moving to New York, but when a Manhattan theater pulled out and "Another Place, Another Time" debuted on March 9, that idea evaporated as far as the Killer was concerned. Though it would only nudge the ceiling of the pop singles chart, the song, backed by surprised and glowing reviews in trade magazines, moved efficiently to the fourth spot on the country charts where it would stay for 17 weeks. (Jerry Lee's previous country hit had been "Pen and Paper," the b-side to "Hit the Road, Jack" in 1964. It had reached #36.) Smash Records took out an ad in the trade papers declaring "Jerry Lee Lewis Has A Smash" — a crowing announcement that they'd waited a long time to make. Back home in Memphis, he had some work to do. If not reflecting the mania of a decade earlier, the times were nonetheless brimming with a sense of purpose for Jerry Lee who, while keeping an eye on the endless road, was genuinely excited to return to Columbia recording studio. There, Kennedy and Kilroy, given a couple of months to consider and solicit, had a new batch of songs waiting. On

Tuesday, April 16 Jerry Lee cut eight new tunes. *Another Place, Another Time* was released two months later, on June 29.

For all intents and purposes a rebirth for Jerry Lee, the album wouldn't convince pop listeners yet of the Killer's resurgence — it peaked in August at #172 on the *Billboard* album charts — but sent a careful, warmly-toned message to his country audience: "Hat in hand, I'm here to play some songs for you if you'd be kind enough to listen." They did. More importantly, they bought. *Another Place, Another Time* rose to the third spot on the *Billboard* Top Country Albums chart and stayed in the top 50 for over seven months. If his storming ego hadn't been all the while predicting it, the Killer himself wouldn't have believed it.

Another Place, Another Time is one of Jerry Lee Lewis' great albums, and one of the era's great country albums.

The lead track has become nearly as synonymous with his name as "Whole Lotta Shakin' Goin' On." Inspired by a beer ad and allegedly written in haste, Glenn Sutton's "What's Made Milwaukee Famous (Has Made A Loser Out Of Me)" is a classic: hard-bitten, funny, and wrapped up as a hook-laden sing-along perfect for any bar or lonely apartment. Renowned for his "countrypolitan" songwriting success, Sutton single-handedly revived Jerry Lee's career with this song; released on June 8, it reached #2 on the country singles chart and stayed there for two triumphant weeks (aided by Smash's winking promotional tie-in, a six-pack of Schlitz sent to all "cooperating" radio stations). Sold by Kennedy's chiming guitar lead and Charlie McCoy's camp-fire harmonica, the opening sends the tune on its gentle, self-mocking way. The arrangement, including a woodblock rather than a snare, is prime honky-tonk: no instrument dominates, all complement, including Jerry Lee's piano flourishes that he employs minimally and for comic effect, imitating the bar's "swinging doors." As good a hook is Jerry Lee's vocal: he gets inside the humor, but bends it around the lyric's genuine regret in a way that makes his delivery both knowing and naked. His vocal soaring up an octave at moving points (to become a drunken affectation within a few years) contributes to the song's emotional authenticity. Everyone involved with the recording must have known that it would be a hit. "What's Made Milwaukee Famous (Has Made A Loser Out Of Me)" is irresistible, a song you can't believe didn't exist before.

The rest of *Another Time, Another Place* is nearly as strong. Among the more memorable touches on this album and the several to follow is Jerry Lee's one-two-three-four piano introductions: the perfect no bullshit lead-in to his songs' misery and misgivings; they always call to my mind Jerry Rivers' fiddle openings of many of Hank Williams' tunes (and call ahead to Dee Dee Ramone's one-two-three-four count-downs opening the Ramones' songs). The band's playing is strong and tasteful on each song. There are no stylistic anxieties among musicians, as everyone knows his job and performs with grace, particularly Gail Davies, whose bona fide, evocative steel guitar playing had been absent on Jerry Lee's records to this point, and Buddy Harman and Kenneth Buttrey, who offer refined percussion.

Jerry Chestnut comes through with two more barroom anthems, "Play Me A Song I Can Cry To" and "On The Back Row." On songs like these, and on "Before The Next Teardrop Falls," "All The Good Is Gone," and Merle Haggard's "I'm A Lonesome Fugitive," Jerry Lee doesn't simply sing well, he sings as if he is curious enough about the words and the characters in the songs — and, by extension, the human condition that they inhabit — to sympathize and, given his thousands of hours loitering, reflecting, and sinning in bars and nightclubs, to empathize with them. This is the kind of emotional generosity that had been largely absent in his recordings in the decade. It can't be that he so invests these songs with care and attention solely because of his concern that they chart well, or that his mulish country audience and dj's get what they demand of their revered form; these songs sound like they genuinely matter to Jerry Lee. Perhaps he needed to step away from the noisiness of rock & roll touring — and who knows what promises it was keeping these days for him anyway, except for the adrenaline rush and the young thighs in bed. Maybe he needed to step quietly and gracefully into the more decorous shape of country music with its long tradition and, startled and pleased, discover that he fit there.

He hit the road in the South, Midwest, and Southwest. "I started in it and I'm in it now," he said of country music, somewhat disingenuously. "But I still have to do all the rockers in the act . . . I give them entertainment, a show. I can tell just by looking at an audience just what they'll want and I tailor my numbers to that." The tension between country and rock & roll would forever come to define Jerry Lee, and not always for the better, as a string of disgruntled audiences would prove in the near future. Ornery to the core, he could or would never commit fully to either camp. The sparks as Ernest Tubb rubbed against Chuck Berry created excitement and danger, but a few inevitably fell unseen to the floor and started a fire that would threaten to consume the Killer at both ends. The carefully handled tensions were overt: for every fiddle-backed appearance on *Hee Haw* or humble presentation on a country music awards show, there were appearances like his 1971 spot on the *Glen Campbell Goodtime Hour* when he played "Blue Suede Shoes" and "Rock 'n' Roll Is Here To Stay" in a pink sport jacket in front of a costumed cast straight out of a 1950s sock hop.

"The man who boasted that he fooled the country audience into financing his career revival took delight in frustrating audiences who'd come to see him rock 'n' roll," Peter Doggett observes in *Are You Ready for the Country*. "He'd rouse a crowd to the point of hysteria, then reel off a succession of country ballads. If his fans were too narrow-minded to know that his taste was as broad as his ego, then they deserved a little provocation." Such provocations would become career-defining, and career-damaging. In (of all places) Hamburg in 1977, he'd nearly start a riot by forcing country songs onto an impatient German crowd still channeling black leather and pomade.

But for now Jerry Lee was sky-high glad, and not only from pharmaceuticals. He was back on the charts, *Cashbox* was lauding him and his commercial resurgence, his concert paydays were fat and regular. In mid-August he ducked into Columbia Studio to record three new tracks, and in October/November a dozen more. Another single and album were quickly sketched out by Smash executives. As it would turn out, *Another Time, Another Place* had provided the essential blueprint for the next half-decade's worth of albums for Jerry Lee. Between one-night stands, extended tours, awards shows, and increasing television appearances (including *The Joey Bishop Show*, *This Is Tom*

Jones, The Monkees' 33 1/3 Special, and *The Mike Douglas Show*), Smash pumped Killer country into the market. On September 28 came "She Still Comes Around (To Love What's Left Of Me)" and on December 28, "To Make Love Sweeter For You." On February 8, 1969 *She Still Comes Around (To Love What's Left Of Me)* debuted on the country album charts, eventually rising to #12 (it peaked at #149 on the pop charts). "To Make Love Sweeter For You" would become Jerry Lee's first #1 single since "Great Balls Of Fire" in 1958, with "She Still Comes Around" peaking at #2. Jerry Lee Lewis was now absurdly bankable. In September, he inked a fresh four-year contract with Mercury.

Short of moving to Nashville, he embraced the Music City formula and audience it served. "I'd like to think that we were recording stuff they wanted to hear and buy," Jerry Kennedy says. "I think that the songs were that good. Timing probably had a lot to do with it, but we just couldn't do anything wrong for a while. His audience was just hungry for some Jerry Lee Lewis country product." When *Another Place, Another Time* finally hit a quarter-million in sales, the Chicago office noticed. "They called me and asked me to check on what pop stations were playing it, because it *couldn't* be selling that many country. And it was not playing on pop anywhere. It was all country radio that was doing the job." It could have been a dicey move on Jerry Lee's part. "You can't fake country people out," songwriter Harlan Howard once said. "If you say something they won't understand, they won't listen again. That's the beauty of country songs, they don't mystify you." Kennedy felt no skepticism on the part of the country audience toward Jerry Lee. "He sounded so much at home it sounded like that's where he'd been all his life," he says.

With its evocative photo of a despondent Killer in a decrepit hotel room, *She Still Comes Around (To Love What's Left Of Me)* was another confident blend of honky-tonk and tear-in-beer ballads. "Jerry was one of the easiest people I ever worked with," says Kennedy, who's worked with plenty on both sides of the studio console, from the Statler Brothers and Kris Kristofferson to Elvis and Bob Dylan. "I've heard a lot of stories of how he butted head with other people, but we always got along great. I didn't spend a lot of time socializing with him. He would come to town, come into my office, and we'd listen to songs, and then we'd go into the studio and record. And then he would go home. Man, he was such a quick study. He learned 'She Even Woke Me Up To Say Goodbye' and did that cut of it after hearing the song one time. He really is a genius."

Standouts this time around included the title song, "To Make Love Sweeter For You," and "Today I Started Loving You Again" (another Merle Haggard tune, confirming now the tradition that Jerry Lee was mining), each song ably showcasing Jerry Lee's newly acquired expressive depth. Provided essentially by the same players on *Another Place, Another Time*, the musicianship was accomplished and wholly supportive of Jerry Lee's interpretations. He rocked the piano a bit harder this time around with "Let's Talk About Us," a rereading of his long-forgotten Sun single from 1959, and "Louisiana Man," though the arrangements were more buttoned-up than the Real Wild Child would've submitted to a decade or so earlier.

The most powerful song on *She Still Comes Around (To Love What's Left Of Me)* is "There Stands The Glass," the Webb Pierce hit from 1953 and one of the all-time classic drinking songs, so controversial at its release that it was

banned on some radio stations. It must be that Jerry Lee
— who offers one of his strongest vocal performances,
control teetering on collapse — felt close to the lyrics.
Maybe too close.

> There stands the glass
> That will ease all my pain . . .
> There stands the glass
> That will hide all my tears
> That will drown all my fears . . .
> I'm wond'ring where you are tonight,
> Wond'ring if you're all right.

His alcoholism was no longer the forgivable partygoer
it had been for years; it was now the spiteful guest that
wouldn't leave, wrecking dusks and dawns alike. In a
couple of years, faced with collapsing griefs and guilt, Jerry
Lee Lewis would swear off the bottle. But he wouldn't stay
dry for long.

June, 1969. Woodstock was ushering in a new era and
closing another, and Jerry Lee was benighted by *Billboard*
as "Country Music Artist of the Year." His touring fees
increased, as did his appearances on major network
television shows. That year also saw a surprising rebirth.
Shelby Singleton had blown off the dust from the boxes
of Sun master tapes newly purchased from Sam Phillips,
and he was ready to cash in. Hearing Jerry Lee's last Sun
sessions from August of 1963, Singleton must've shook his
head in disbelief: he wasn't listening to the Killer's recent
recordings with Kennedy but it sure as hell sounded that
way. Between 1969 and 1973, as Jerry Lee was riding high
on the country charts, Singleton would release seven

"brand new" singles culled from those '63 sessions. These Sun International discs would prove lively companions to the still-charting Smash sides: "Invitation To Your Party" reached #6 in August of 1969, while "One Minute Past Eternity" reached #2 in November. Singleton pinched himself while Phillips could only shake his head. And Jerry Lee didn't need any more evidence that the gods were now smiling down on him favorably after ten long years.

So, he kept on going. In April, Smash released *Jerry Lee Lewis Sings The Country Music Hall Of Fame*, a two-volume set of covers that he knocked out in a mammoth two-day session at Columbia, a label-described "thank you" to his dollar-waving fans ("Country music has always been Jerry's music," Stuart Lewis wrote with a straight face on the album jacket.) The album's song selection was broad and unsurprising, and the swift recordings of made-to-order arrangements didn't allow Jerry Lee much of an opportunity for nuance. But the LP did its job and his fans were indeed grateful, sending *Vol. I* to the second spot on the country albums charts and *Vol. II* to the fifth.

Together, a lively but uneven album of duets with his sister, Linda Gail, appeared in September, highlighted by the barnstorming opener, John Prine's "Milwaukee Here I Come," during which an arms-folded Jerry Lee demands that his fans choose between them Opry stars and him. That same month he played the Rock & Roll Revival Show in Toronto, doing his thing with Gene Vincent, Bo Diddley, Chuck Berry, and Little Richard, along with a woolly-bearded John Lennon and a wailing Yoko Ono. Sign of the times. In May of 1970, Jerry Lee and the Memphis Beats played a month's worth of shows at the International Hotel in Las Vegas; in August, a decently produced live album appeared that focused on the country performances, leaving dozens of rock & roll numbers in the can (to dutifully crop up on bootlegs). *Jerry Lee Lewis Live At The International, Las Vegas* was another commercial winner. His eighth album in two and a half years to chart on the *Billboard* Top Country Albums chart, it would stay there for nearly half a year.

Those albums were placeholders for *She Even Woke Me To Say Goodbye*, recorded in October and November of 1969 at Fred Foster's Monument Studio in Nashville. Released in January of 1970, Jerry Lee's last great pure country album is the apex of his resurgence, the well-chosen, warmly recorded songs accumulating into a rich statement of purpose, as if each cut was measured and made by the same breath. Even *Another Place, Another Time* and *She Still Comes Around (To Love What's Left Of Me)* fall short of the kind of devotion to the rich traditions and history of honky-tonk music that this album reveals. It's a respectful record, but the deference stems from the native love and passion of the musicians and so it's lived-in and organic; there's nothing too earnest or reverent here. That it's a respectful record made by Jerry Lee Lewis means that he's still the center of attention — as he crows about in one song — but his ego is complemented by the greatness of the music.

Recorded at the tail end of the turbulent Sixties, the album leads off with a tune written by a man who would become a Seventies icon. "Once More With Feeling" was an early Kris Kristofferson song (co-written with Shel Silverstein). An archetypal struggling Music Row tunesmith, Kristofferson had recently written the Roger Miller hit "Me And Bobby McGee," and in a heady couple of years would see a clutch of his unique songs reach the charts in the hands of able artists. "There had never been a country songwriter quite like him," historian Bill Malone wrote. Kristofferson's blend of musical classicism and progressive lyrics helped open up country music subject matter with "intimate, sensuous language that had been rare." Kristofferson was thrilled to land material on Jerry Lee's albums. "I consider Jerry Lee Lewis one of the great singers of all time," Kristofferson said. "Put him up there with opera singers. This guy's a natural resource who is inclined to self destruct. He had a way of transforming my songs into something I couldn't believe I was hearing." Jerry Lee invests "Once More With Feeling" with the sorrow barely masked by the song's timeless metaphor: the singer is aching to rediscover the magic that's disappeared between himself and his girl, and he offers that they sing a duet "from the top" to find the strength and intimacy that's gone. Whether Jerry Lee was channeling the grief over the Lost Weekend that was the 1960s, or the grief over his disastrous marriage is unclear: I feel the sincerity with which he moves along this stately, quietly devastating song. It was another inevitable hit, reaching the second spot on the country charts in February and staying for 14 weeks.

Jerry Lee dug deep into his weather-beaten bag of musical loves on this album. Chuck Berry ("Brown-Eyed Handsome Man"), Jimmie Rodgers ("Waiting For A Train"), and again Merle Haggard ("Workin' Man Blues") receive his honky-tonk blessing, as do a handful of strong originals highlighted by the title track (a #2 hit in the fall), Glenn Sutton's "My Only Claim To Fame," and Don Chapel's "When The Grass Grows Over Me." *She Even Woke Me To Say Goodbye* was another top 10 country album hit for Jerry Lee. After the release, Smash Records folded into parent company Mercury, where Jerry Lee would stay for 11 more years.

As the Seventies dawned, the Killer was standing tall in public profile, but staggering privately. 1970 would rain down a series of blows that bruised his ego and his confidence, driving him closer to his God than ever before, but bringing into aching relief the contradictions that threatened to lay him out.

Backstage: Late summer. Myra hires a private investigator to follow her husband and to detail his mounting and blatant offenses against their marriage vows. The P.I. fills books full of evidence. In November, Myra files for divorce, citing not only emotional abandonment in the form of long absences and countless infidelities but dire and violent physical and mental abuse. The divorce becomes final on May 12, 1971.

In September of 1969, Jerry Lee's beloved mother Mamie endures an operation for lung cancer. She is seriously ill for months as she battles treatments that fail to stop the spread of the cancer. She dies at the age of 59 on April 20, 1971.

On December 8, 1970, Walter Cronkite announces on the *CBS Evening News* that Jerry Lee Lewis has abandoned rock & roll for country and gospel music, and that he will cancel all nightclub dates. In a press release, booking agent Ray Brown states solemnly that Jerry Lee, who'd been averaging hundreds of shows a year for more than a decade, will drastically curtail his performances, work only Thursday through Saturday nights, and drop several gospel songs into his act. Earlier that month, Jerry Lee swore off drink.

The war was on between his Pentecostal conscience and his cock, between his liver and his ever-steadying hand, between his scruples and Mercury's bottom line.

Around this time he conceived of a special project that must've felt preordained. *In Loving Memories: The Jerry Lee Lewis Gospel Album* appeared on the first day of 1971, as Jerry Lee's mother lay ill and as his struggles to sober up were becoming daily theater. "All his life Jerry Lee has had a real personal interest in Gospel music," Linda Gail wrote decorously on the back jacket. "In fact, the first song he ever sang in public was in the little Assembly of God Church, right here in Ferriday, Louisiana." Choosing her words carefully, she adds, "Jerry Lee has always played and sung his own type of Gospel music. He was doing a mixture of Rock and Roll, Negro spirituals and Blues — all in one — and with a beat. They just couldn't understand or accept it back then. Things are different now."

Jerry Lee and Linda Gail manned the boards themselves on this thinly-produced but affecting and sincere record. Thinking secularly, Jerry Lee kept some of the bucks in the family, recording three songs written by his sister and her off-and-on husband, the Killer's old buddy Cecil Harrelson. The remaining material was comprised of well-known, bedrock Christian gospel songs. The arrangements in the hands of the familiar Nashville studio crowd weren't much different from his country albums, aided and abetted (and given God-fearing legitimacy) here and there by backing vocals from the Jordanaires and the Nashville Sounds. The material moves between measured, piously paced slow numbers like "Gather 'Round Children" to tambourine-quickened Holy Roller ovations like A.E. Brumley's "I'll Fly Away." Jerry Lee sounds fully committed.

In Loving Memories is a mightily devout-sounding record. Jerry Lee reaches some poignant moments in his phrasing when he allows himself to face his guilt and moral failings; the staggering "He Looked Beyond My Fault" features an especially moving vocal, flamboyant but honest. Later in the album, when he sings that he's longing for home and sends it heavenward with an aching falsetto cry, it's pretty convincing stuff. Elsewhere, as in "The Old Rugged Cross," he sounds stiff and mannered, learning lines for a character he doesn't fully understand or trust. But it was the kind of album that Jerry Lee needed to make at this time in his troubled life. Tolerant Mercury executives lukewarmly promoted the latest from their chart-busting artist. His fans, especially those accustomed to hearing the phrase "Jesus Christ" popping up reverently in song, dutifully bought the album and sent it to #18 on the country album charts.

An occasional right-hand flourish can be heard on the album fighting its way against the biblical tide, sounding like the half-grinning smartass in the back pew, popping gum and mentally undressing the shapely parishioners around him. A telling document from this era is an all-gospel show that Jerry Lee performed and recorded at a Church of God in suburban Memphis in December of 1970 ("probably the Barton Heights congregation with which he was formally affiliated," Stephen R. Tucker notes). The tensions between his profane and sacred selves find a predictable home in the lighted and sacramental stage. Loyal Ken Lovelace was in the band, as was Jerry Lee, Jr. on drums, as the Killer earnestly performed 20 hardcore gospel songs in an hour, a man desperately balancing his twin desires.

Consigned to the shelf by Mercury, released decades

later on a Bear Family box set, the performance remains a curious footnote in Jerry Lee's career. Introducing "On The Jericho Road," Jerry Lee says to the evangelical throng, "Well, I'll tell you one thing, this old-time religion is good. I believe in old-time religion, that's the way I was raised. Didn't live it for a long time but thank God I'm on the right track now. For quite a while there I had the right string but the wrong yo-yo. But right now I got what it takes!" He then lets out a laugh that even the most pious couldn't tell was grace or lechery. To some genuine "Hallelujahs" and a smattering of murmurs, Jerry Lee launches the high-spirited number, followed swiftly by an equally forceful "I'll Fly Away."

He had the pedigree, of course. In addition to his genuine sense of and belief in the sacred, he'd grown up surrounded by the gospel spirit, in song and in family. His uncle Lee Calhoun was an influential, wealthy, mid-century supporter of Ferriday's first Assembly of God Church; televangelist and preacher Jimmy Lee Swaggart is his cousin. "If white sanctified music was the music of the grave," wrote Nick Tosches, "black sanctified music was the music of the Judgment Day quaking that would shake and sunder the grave. Of the few country singers who have felt and foreseen and conveyed that shaking, Jerry Lee Lewis comes foremost to mind." Listen to him sing "That Lucky Old Sun" alone at the piano at the cusp of his career, filtering Tin Pan Alley through the sanctified:

> Oh, Lord above, don't you hear me cryin'
> Tears are rollin' down my eyes
> Send in a cloud with a silver linin'
> Take me to paradise.

Austin journalist Michael Corcoran makes the convincing case that Jerry Lee's early, formative influences likely included Arizona Dranes, a blind Pentecostal gospel pianist from Texas. "She was the first musical star of the Pentecostal religion, the first gospel pianist to record and be credited with inventing 'the gospel beat' that grew into rock & roll," Corcoran says, adding that he feels Dranes influenced all gospel piano players. "Also, she was based in Memphis during the 1930s and 1940s, putting the words of Bishop Mason to music. Many of those songs were also sung in Assemblies of God services in Arkansas and Louisiana." Jerry Lee didn't have to dig too deeply to find native encouragement and inspiration, and as always was trespassing the line between the sacred and the secular.

Legendary Memphis producer and musician Jim Dickinson feels that one of Jerry Lee's musical signatures, an essential ingredient in early rock & roll, might have had its origins in the church. In his early songs at Sun, Jerry Lee would often interrupt the standard boogie-woogie left-hand progression by omitting the seventh and repeating the fifth and sixth, creating a repetitive, driving, quasi-menacing momentum. (Listen to "Hand Me Down My Walking Cane" from 1957, or the rumbling opening of "Whole Lotta Shakin' Goin' On" from *"Live" At The Star-Club*.) "That really was revolutionary, almost inexplicable," Dickinson claims. "Maybe Ella Mae Morse, maybe Moon Mullican had done it, but not in a way where it became the propelling force of the song. Rock & roll piano up to that point had been defined by Roscoe Gordon, Ike Turner, and to an extent Ray Charles. None of them were doing that. Even Little Richard, as primitive as he plays, wasn't doing that shuffle." He adds, "There was something in Jerry Lee that didn't want to play that seventh, and that's the church. Certainly in white spiritual music you have to avoid sevenths. Emmylou Harris will fire a musician who plays a seventh! There's something that is secular in making that seventh in the change."

I can picture the Memphis congregation clapping along to the rousing "I'm In The Gloryland Way." I can also imagine them wrinkling their faces at the splayed legs, the self-referencing, the sly half-grins, whispering to each other as they left the church, "And what on earth's his son on?"

"The weeks that Jerry Lee dedicated to Christ mark the apogee of his career in country music," Peter Doggett observes. "The twelve months before had been the most successful of his career. He'd spent two years wooing the country audience, making all the expected career moves. But the straitjacket soon began to loosen. Even his calmest performances offered clues that the real Jerry Lee — a hell-raising, ego-charged son of a gun — hadn't been subdued." Within two months of the Memphis church performance Jerry Lee was in the studio "Comin' Back For More." A month later he was singing about being a "Foolish Kind Of Man." By June he was shoutin' and a-shakin' almost off his bat after a "Big Blon' Baby." By summer he'd gone back to his sinning ways, upping his nightclub appearances, playing rock & roll and garlanding the songs with naughty asides, hitting the sauce hard, and running around with a young, pretty employee from the Memphis Sheriff's Office named Jaren whom he'd soon knock up. In the fall, he'd grudgingly marry her.

Fast forward: February, 1979. Jerry Lee is performing at the Louisiana State University Assembly Center in Baton

Rouge. At the end of the set he looks up and is surprised to see Jimmy Lee Swaggart on stage, beckoning to him. Wasted in the stratosphere, Jerry Lee barely recognizes the blur of a cousin who stops the show, ducks the promoters, sends away grumbling fans waiting for the second set, and drags him to the safety of home and family. The man who would in a few years decry rock & roll as "the new pornography" offers Jerry Lee safety and succor. Though he stays with Swaggart for a week, eating well, drying out, reading and discussing the Bible and reckoning with his fate, like all attempts at finding a core grace in the Killer, this sojourn with a well-intentioned preacher fails. Within weeks he's drinking excessively, skipping shows, and skidding cars.

"I'm a rock 'n' roll singer," Jerry Lee wrote in his autobiography. "I like good whiskey, good looking women and good music. . . . When the Lord's book is opened, we will stand before Him and be judged. God gave me my talent. He will judge me. No man or woman can. I don't question God, but I don't think I'll have much of an argument with God. Satan don't scare me worth a damn.

"Satan won't bother me."

When he was off the road, between benders, away from the hospital and wedding chapel, and avoiding the U.S. Government, Jerry Lee ducked in and out of studios. The market needed feeding. He spent the 1970s cutting a series of albums that satisfied the Nashville formula: *There Must Be More To Love Than This* (1971); *Touching Home* (1971); *Would You Take Another Chance On Me* (1971); *Who's Gonna Play This Old Piano* (1972); *Killer Rocks On* (1973); *Sometimes A Memory Ain't Enough* (1973); *Southern Roots* (1973); *I-40 Country* (1974); *Sessions*

(1974); *Boogie Woogie Country Man* (1975); *Odd Man In* (1975); *Country Class* (1976); *Country Memories* (1977) . . . Many were uneven, a couple (*Southern Roots, Sessions*) were well-promoted all-star events touted as comebacks. Nearly all were marked by Jerry Lee's increasingly lackadaisical, whiskey-scorched performances, lesser and lesser *Billboard* sales, and gradually sinking spirits.

In the studio and on stage he could still focus and pull out genuinely great performances when he cared to, when the words cold-cocked him with their honesty. *There Must Be More To Love Than This*, the follow-up to *In Loving Memories*, follows the prescription for the most part, but offers a trio of songs that plugs Jerry Lee into humming current. "One More Time" begins brutally: "Mistakes, I know I've made them," he admits, but then surprises with the next line, "and you don't know how much I hate them," before shrugging, "But that's me darlin', and I don't guess ol' Jerry will ever change." It's a beautifully sung song in its balance of egoism and compromise, and Ned Davis' steel guitar mourns the valid regrets at its center. Jerry Chestnut offers another winner, the bar ballad "Home Away From Home" that opens with the unforgettable line, "It all began the day my conscience died." No doubt on his dark days the Killer felt that that would be his epitaph. Sentiments like these allow Jerry Lee to find in melody and word the ways to utter what most confounds him. The album isn't entirely introspective: the jazz standard "Sweet Georgia Brown" is one of the fastest tunes that Jerry Lee had cut in a while, and his grinning band can barely keep up. His playing is superb and effortless (as is Lovelace's high-speed fiddle playing) and he's clearly enjoying himself kicking up his heels.

As the factory ground on over the years, it became

harder to locate genuine greatness in Jerry Lee's perfor-
mances, but amidst the worn clichés, Kris Kristofferson's
"Help Me Make It Through The Night," Jimmie Rodgers'
"Mother, Queen Of My Hearts," the aching "Touching
Home," "Another Hand Shakin' Goodbye," "Would You
Take A Chance On Me," the gospel rave-up "Jesus Is
On The Mainline," and Tom T. Hall's wry "I Can Still
Hear The Music In The Restroom" (in which Jerry Lee
owns up to snorting blow) are all lively and memorable
performances spanning remorse, humor, salvation, and
bitterness. "A Damn Fine Country Song" from *Odd Man
In* is the inevitable statement of purpose rescued from
self-absorption by a liquored-up, bemused bout of rueful
candor. After Jerry Lee's move to Elektra Records in 1979,
the albums became slicker and shinier. An eccentric take
on Johnny Cash's "Folsom Prison Blues" on *Killer Country*
(1980) works despite a time-stamp disco beat that pulses
mechanically beneath it, failing to drain the blood from
Jerry Lee's playing. "Thirty-Nine and Holding" from the
same album gave the Killer a hit, and yet another signature tune. He sings it well, trusting the song's bemused,
self-mocking appeal.

As Jerry Lee aged, as his alcoholism and chemical depen-
dencies grew worse, his performances became erratic.
On occasion, his voice, though rough, was able to divine
an emotional depth that was "far from unbecoming," as
Colin Escott puts it, revealing "a poignancy bordering on
desperation on some cuts." Yet he was too often indulgent,
singing sentimentally, metamorphosing into the braying
drunk at the end of the bar who believes that his woes are
unique, the booze lifting up him and his tales in gales of
over-emotion. (Listen to "I Was Sorta Wonderin'" from

Boogie Woogie Country Man.) He'd slur his words, his producers forced to compensate with strings and loudly mixed backing singers. He was canceling shows and blowing off recording sessions. Jimmy Gutterman once noted that "A good lyric could make Jerry Lee the singer sound far more trenchant emotionally than Jerry Lee the man." "I Wish I Was Eighteen Again" from his 1979 eponymous Elektra debut and the title track to *When Two Worlds Collide* (1980) show what the right ballad can become in his hands.

Three songs in particular — their origins and recordings spanning a quarter century — reign among Jerry Lee's very best. "I'd Do it All Again" from *Killer Country* is fabulous autobiography, a hard-bitten tale of vexed triumphs that sounds as if Jerry Lee was completely wasted when he sang it. Whatever the circumstances, the vocal he turns in is loose, weary, but commanding, singed with both remorse and defiance. "That Kind Of Fool" from *Odd Man In* is one of the great performances of his career. Written by Mack Vickery, who had auditioned at Sun Records as a 19 year old and who would write strong material for Jerry Lee in the Seventies, the song encompasses in two and a half minutes everything appealing and problematic about the Killer's persona. I'd argue that his singing here is the very essence of his career and talent: regret, denial, and grudging acceptance, each rubbing up against self-importance, each risking self-pity. The tune was important to Jerry Lee; Escott notes that Jerry Lee sent a personal telegram to Mercury urging the label to release it as single. He would revive the song often, publicly and privately, including a compelling version in 2003 that was later adorned with a gruff, lived-in, fitting duet from Keith Richards. The masterstroke idea appeared on *Last*

Man Standing, Jerry Lee's hyped and commercially successful album from 2006. Also on that collection is Mick Jagger's "Evening Gown," an under-recognized beauty that Jerry Lee sings in tandem with the Rolling Stones frontman, who wittily, and wisely, lets the Killer keep the spotlight. The performance is charming, a tale of the trials and pleasures of aging sung by a bruised man in his Sixties. Craggy around the edges and utterly true in the center, it's a gem, quite possibly the last one we'll get from the man.

Jerry Lee's private life spiraled wildly in the 1970s and 1980s, an opera of blur and clarity. The real loosening began with the tragic death of his drug-abusing son Jerry Lee, Jr. in a car accident on November 13, 1973. Funeral services were held at the Assembly of God Church in Ferriday. In the span of a decade, he'd lost two sons and his mother. A week later, he bought a Rolls Royce limousine and hit the road, turning to sensation and footlights to help him deal with the chaos of grief.

The fall of 1976 included two episodes that have grown mythic with the passing of time. With federal charges of tax evasion rapidly closing in on him, and with his country records stubbornly refusing to cross over to pop and so dying a slow death, a drunk and rash Jerry Lee shot his bass player "Butch" Owens in the chest. He claims that he was aiming for a Coke bottle across the room. Owens survived after emergency surgery; Jerry Lee was fined for shooting a firearm inside the city limits — he should have been fined for reckless self-destruction. ("The moral of the story is not to have a hair trigger pistol," Jerry Lee offers, helpfully.) Then, on November 23, he was arrested outside of the gates at Elvis Presley's Graceland mansion.

He was drunk and waving a pistol. Earlier that day he'd overturned his Roll Royce after dropping off his young daughter Lori at kindergarten — tragedy averted — and continued to drink through the afternoon and evening, before he left Bad Bob's Vapors Club and headed down Elvis Presley Boulevard. The Killer was angry, embarrassed, grieving private and public anguishes, and lost. What has been cast as one of the epic adventures in Jerry Lee's life stemmed from profound but simple addictions, what Jerry Lee himself had sung dejectedly about a couple of years earlier as "the alcohol of fame."

Vapors would forever cloud his vision, judgment, and urges toward benevolence — both to his career and to his loved ones, many of whom were fleeing him at this point. On February 3, 1978 he entered the Mid-South Hospital in Memphis for alcohol addiction and psychiatric care, the beginning of decades worth of hospital stays for health issues minor and grave. In June of 1981 he suffered a severe setback, collapsing at home, and was rushed to the hospital with a tear in his stomach lining. He endured two lengthy surgeries and was in intensive care for two months battling peritonitis and a series of grim infections. (The single released two days after he was discharged? "I'd Do It All Again.")

In April of 1985, he was back in the hospital, this time with bleeding ulcers. He spent three days in intensive care, and was released a week later. But in November, weeks after taping an appearance for a Johnny Cash Christmas show on CBS, he was rushed back to Methodist Hospital with a recurrence of ulcers. Surgeons removed one-third of his stomach in a four-hour operation, afterward warning him that the drinking, smoking, and drug abuse had to end. By December, he was whoring it up at Hernando's

Hideaway Club in Memphis, where his wife caught him with another woman.

At least this wife — Kerrie, his sixth — was alive. His fourth wife Jaren had drowned in a swimming pool in 1982. His fifth wife Shawn died a year later in bed next to him, fluid having built up in her lungs, the result of an apparent suicide from sleeping pills. (Jim Dickinson: "Jerry Lee took the same pills she did. He lived, she died. It was God's will.") He was acquitted of any wrongdoing in these deaths, but the Killer sobriquet assumed new and notorious shadings. He'd always fought women — literally in bruising assaults, figuratively as confounding temptresses — and his woeful history with them has been harder to ignore than mammoth tax evasion and reckless good ol' boy gun-shooting. His reputation as a man befouled, he'd withdraw to his ranch in Nesbit, Mississippi, and briefly in the mid-Nineties to a home in Dublin, Ireland. The years came and went: Kerrie bore him a son in 1987; she and Jerry Lee divorced in 2005. Jerry Lee now lives at his ranch with daughter Phoebe, who manages his twilit career. For a while they'd opened the home to eager fans for tours, another novel way to pay back Uncle Sam, but this ceased after the divorce from Kerrie. A sign at his gate posted by "Ranch Security" warns away any fans and visitors who might wish to ogle his car collection and piano-shaped swimming pool, or who might want to knock one back and otherwise commune with the Killer.

Music has always been his salvation, and he would continue to tour internationally (damaging his itineraries with cancellations), appear on television, and release the odd single or album. He watched over the years as cousin Mickey Gilley rose to popularity and as cousin Jimmy Lee Swaggart fell from grace. He listened as the likes of

Gary Stewart took his place at the barstool and on the *Billboard* charts, crooning honky-tonk drinking songs with authority. Jerry Lee himself would periodically come into and out of sharp focus in pop culture: in 1989 with the release of *Great Balls Of Fire*, Hollywood's version of his life-story, in 1995 with *Youngblood*, a slick and bloodless "comeback" album, and in the form of continuing, respectful, and welcome digital reissues of his work across his five-decade career. As the years passed, Jerry Lee's ledger and heart grew heavy with sin. "He's Pentecostal," says Jim Dickinson, "He's afraid to die."

"I don't think I'll have much of an argument with God . . ."

Southern Gothic fiction writer Flannery O'Connor writes of the key gesture that a character makes that reveals the true heart of the story. "This would have to be an action or a gesture which was both totally right and totally unexpected," she wrote. "It would have to be one that was both in character and beyond character; it would have to suggest both the world and eternity." A devout Catholic, O'Connor was considering her characters in the context of the everlasting. But a key gesture, revealing that which is least dispensable about us as human beings, always has worldly origins.

On January 20, 1973 Jerry Lee appeared on the Grand Ole Opry, an act of consecration on the part of the country music establishment, an act of revolution on the part of the Killer. The Nashville institution was nearly a half-century old by the time it got around to showcasing Jerry Lee, and legend has it that he was asked by Opry folk to keep his language clean and to play only country songs. ("What country?" Jerry Lee asked, smirking.) Legend has also supplied the inevitable punch line to those impractical requests. "The Opry wasn't cutting edge," songwriter and host Bill Anderson acknowledged. "It wasn't designed to be cutting edge. The Opry was comfort." Jerry Lee was in his element: the invited center-of-attention courting the concerns of those fearing what the hell he might do next.

Relishing the sanctifying spotlight, wearing a long, crushed-velvet jacket and pointed leather boots, Jerry Lee opened with "Another Place, Another Time" but was soon barreling through "What'd I Say" and "Mean Woman Blues." Versions of "I Can't Seem To Say Goodbye" and "Once More With Feeling" shuddered next to a stomping five-minute medley of "Whole Lotta Shakin' Goin' On," "Workin' Man Blues," and "Rock Around The Clock." You get the idea. If the Opry organizers had listened to *"Live" At The Star-Club* they might've had second thoughts about their invitation. At the midway point of the hour-long show, Jerry Lee interrupted proceedings to invite on stage longtime Opry pianist Del Wood, then in her fifties. Jerry Lee cited her as a chief influence early in his career, and together they played an outrageously good ragtime version of "Down Yonder," after which they hugged. In front of a bemused band and a curious but stirred-up audience, a sweating Jerry Lee announced, "Let me tell you something, ladies and gentlemen. I am a rock-'n'-rollin', country-and-western, rhythm-'n-blues *mutha*!"

His key *motherfucking* gesture. At the end of the performance, he warbled a barely controlled "I'm So Lonesome I Could Cry" and it sounded as if he was singing to his career. The show ran 20 minutes over and interrupted Ernest Tubb's *Midnight Jamboree* radio show. Killer wasn't asked back to Ryman Auditorium.

A couple of years later he'd make it official, opening "Boogie Woogie Country Man" with the declaration:

> You can call me country,
> I have been known to be a little wild,
> but I am what I am, doin' the best I can.

LONGING FOR HOME

"I don't regret any of the years that God's let me live on this earth," Jerry Lee wrote in his autobiography. "I've had a wonderful life, a great career. I just want to be remembered for my music." Jerry Lee Lewis was inducted into the Rock and Roll Hall of Fame in 1986, the institution's inaugural year. He was honored along with Sam Phillips, Chuck Berry, James Brown, Ray Charles, Sam Cooke, Fats Domino, the Everly Brothers, Buddy Holly, Little Richard,

Jimmie Rodgers, and Elvis.

What's Jerry Lee Lewis' legacy in country music? He's an interesting figure in that he performed successful, conventional country songs, but he remains an outsider, estranged from the establishment. In *Lost Highway*, Peter Guralnick defines the "Outlaw" tradition. "'Outlaw' is the word that has been used, and abused, to describe the 'new' country music that deviates from the Nashville norm," he wrote in 1979. "The principal way in which this music deviates, ironically enough, is that it is traditional music, which honors roots, black and white, which recognizes Jimmie Rodgers, Ernest Tubb, Hank Williams, and Lefty Frizzell — the pure lineage that runs in an unbroken line of descent though country music." Jerry Lee is rarely considered in the same category as Willie Nelson, Waylon Jennings, or Billy Joe Shaver, long championed as the original Outlaws, nor did he explicitly reject what Guralnick calls "the plasticity of the contemporary Nashville sound." In fact, he was more or less submitting to it by the mid- and late 1970s.

But his rebellious, iconoclastic image and lifestyle modeled indirectly on the Hank Myth, his tackling of songs by Merle Haggard and Kris Kristofferson, his embrace of hard country and honky-tonk, and his fierce individualism point to an outlaw ethos all his own. Jerry Lee might have celebrated the historical tradition of country music, but his country career "could only be ascribed to anachronistic impulse," Guralnick argues, adding, "Perhaps what most connects all the [Outlaw] figures is the strikingly personal way in which they express themselves, with all the feeling and flavor of the blues (Hank Williams' greatest songs were almost without exception blues-inspired), even when the blues form is missing."

Jerry Lee honors that tradition, but his idiosyncratic way of doing so has kept him, in large part, on the outside looking in. "I think at this point he occupies a secondary place in the country music pantheon," says Chet Flippo, longtime music writer and current Editorial Director at Country Music Television. "He seemed to come later to country, and then as a means of career survival. The music he did make remains undeniable and I think it will ultimately earn him a lasting spot as a country great. My sense is that the honky tonk crowd early on warmed to him, didn't care what others thought, and never left him. But the Grand Ole Opry crowd and the Nashville country pillars were not interested." John Lomax III, member of the luminous family of folk and country historians and archivists, declares flatly: "Jerry Lee Lewis belongs in the Hall of Fame, but will never be selected."

Colin Escott wonders if the Killer's independence isn't the crucial reason. "The fact that he's not in the Country Music Hall of Fame despite a prodigious number of hits seems to show what the country establishment thinks of him," Escott acknowledges. Jerry Lee opened an office in Nashville, but he never moved to the city. "He rarely if ever schmoozed around town," Escott continues. "Was he ignored or blackballed because of his marital transgressions or because he'd been a rock 'n' roller? I doubt it. He just went his own way." Shelby Singleton agrees. "It has a lot to do with politics. Jerry *is* noted as a rock & roller, not country," he says, adding, "Many other greats are not in the Hall of Fame."

"It disappoints me," says Jerry Kennedy of Jerry Lee's exclusion. "I think he belongs there. It could be that it's just the attitude of the Nashville Establishment. I'm not familiar with who's on the nominating committee but it takes some real big people to admit that somebody outside of Nashville can be a Hall of Fame member." Kennedy mentions the recently inducted Statler Brothers, who'd steadfastly ignored Nashville's entreaties, refusing to move from their home base of Staunton, Virginia. "Maybe that will open the door for more," he reflects. "But Jerry Lee is *very* Memphis."

Kindred spirit Johnny Cash was tattooed by the River City. "Outlaws, I think that's just another way of saying 'new direction,'" Cash told Patrick Carr. "Y'know, myself, back in '56, I had a hard time breaking into the country music community in Nashville. . . . See, I was one of those Memphis rockabillies — had sideburns — from the Memphis school of Presley and Perkins and Lewis and Orbison and Cash. It was a wonder they even let us in the city limits, the way they looked down on us at the time." Memphis writer Robert Gordon defines the Tennessee division line thus: "Nashville is a company town and Memphis is for renegades." Jim Dickinson picks up the thread, asserting that the Country Music Hall of Fame is plainly afraid of Jerry Lee. "Nashville embraces the corporate, they reject the individual," he says. "They're terrified of him — they may have been afraid of Waylon, but they'll steer clear of Jerry Lee. Rightly so. Who knows what he would do if they inducted him. Think about the acceptance speech!"

Christine Kreyling has called Music Row in Nashville "the Vatican of country music." Jerry Lee didn't genuflect all that often. Ultimately, what his country fans honed in on was the sincerity of his performances, the authenticity of the emotions he traveled through in song. His hero Hank Williams would've probably understood. Explaining his enormous success to Rufus Jarman in oft-quoted comments that were published the month after he died in 1953, Williams said, "It can be explained in one word: sincerity. When a hillbilly sings a crazy song, he feels crazy. When he sings 'I Laid My Mother Away,' he sees her a-laying right there in the coffin. . . . The people who has been raised something like the way the hillbilly has, knows what he is singing about and appreciates it."

"No one was better at mainstream country music, when Jerry Lee Lewis set his mind to do it," argues historian Bill Malone, author of the comprehensive history *Country Music, U.S.A.* "As far as legacy, I think he had more influence than anybody else who was singing at the time. He was a *convincing* performer. He grew up with it, he heard it at home. His songs didn't sound like parodies or pale imitations. They sounded like the real thing. I could see somebody sitting in a honky tonk somewhere nursing a bottle of beer, really absorbed in what he was saying."

"Despite all of the strikes against him, Jerry Lee blazed a bold trail with his country music work, and didn't apologize or seek forgiveness," Chet Flippo feels. "As a result, I think it will stand for what it is — a from-the-heart musical statement from an artist who lives and breathes music and who never thought in terms of musical genres, and throughout his life and career disdained musical categories." Flippo adds, "Remember, he was drummed out of rock & roll and mainstream America after a two-year career, and has spent the rest of his life getting by on the country audience and his die-hard fans.

"His lasting influence is that of the musical free spirit, a talent who truly was bloodied but remained unbowed."

Rock & roll has always loved him, rock & roll always

will. His epochal songs and performances in the Sun years, especially the 1950s, secured his permanent foothold in the foundation. He remains an influence and inspiration.

With his hell-raising, Wild Child spirit, the Killer infused American punk. The work at Sun — and, especially, the primitivism of *"Live" At The Star-Club* — were precursors. Cousins in mayhem in the early and mid-1960s were garage rockers the Sonics, who in the Pacific Northwest were pounding their source material and rudimentary originals into a pulpy mass, sending the studio needles into the distortion-loving red, to the astonishment and irritation of their recording engineers. Musically, the Sonics were a few chucked sharp-edged stones away from Iggy Pop and the Stooges, who built the sturdy bridge to late-Seventies-style punk rock. The lineage is there. On *"Live" At The Star-Club*, Jerry Lee and the Nashville Teens, in cymbal-crashing, stomping 4/4, so destroy and then impudently rebuild the songs that they attack that when the dust settles we have one of the great punk albums. The onstage crash into "Lewis Boogie" calls ahead to the Ramones' onstage crash into, say, "Surfin' Bird" — save for a few million Marshall Amp watts. The performances manhandle each song and turn them inside out until we hear them new again.

Among the many musicians influenced by Jerry Lee in the 1970s were two Los Angeles-based songwriters who discovered themselves at the ground floor of punk. Dave Alvin founded the roots-rock band the Blasters in 1979; John Doe formed seminal punk band X in 1977; both bands, in unique ways, refracted the spirit of the Killer. Doe would portray Myra's father J.W. Brown in *Great Balls Of Fire* in 1989, a very visible way of dramatizing the Killer's enduring impact on the musician. "X was definitely influenced by Jerry Lee," Doe says. "There was a point where you really couldn't get old Fifties rock & roll records, Little Richard, Gene Vincent. And we'd seek them out in thrift stores and places like that. That was the whole point of punk rock, to go back to shorter, faster, less intellectual stuff — even though they could still be poetic — back to the freedom that Jerry Lee had. That was, maybe, a misconception about the resurgence of punk rock. The Ramones were maybe listening to doo-wop, and we were listening to 'Whole Lotta Shakin' Goin' On' and 'Great Balls of Fire'."

X would record a memorably wire-taut, spiky version of "Breathless" in 1983, around the time that they paid Jerry Lee $10,000 to open for them and fellow Californian punks the Minutemen at the Universal Amphitheatre, an hysterical and successful meeting of rock & roll and post-disco anarchy. For X and many other bands, punk was less about radical politics and personal nihilism than it was about demolishing the likes of the Eagles and Fleetwood Mac with the elemental, fierce weapons of early rock & roll. "Punk in America was more musical and less cultural," Doe says. "It was devoted in part to recapturing that feeling of Fifties rock."

Doe was blown away by *"Live" At The Star-Club* when he first got his hands on it. "It's so aggressive and fast, and it's pretty rare on record when you can hear the band trying to stay with the singer!" he laughs. "When I first listened to it, it seemed like after the years of being rejected, having fallen from grace and gone from making ten grand a night to five hundred, he had a huge chip on his shoulder and wanted to prove that he was the baddest rock & roller around. I love the fact that that night at the

Star-Club, Jerry Lee was taking no prisoners, he truly was the Killer." Beyond the astonishing piano playing and the mammoth stage energy, Jerry Lee's greatness stems from his singing, Doe feels. "His voice is second to none. It's incredibly clear and limber. He can do anything."

The Blasters were the first collective of able musicians through which Dave Alvin would filter his love of blues, rockabilly, and country. He remembers Jerry Lee's influence as cultural and historical, as well as musical: as a young boy in the mid-Sixties, unaware of genres or *Billboard* politics, Alvin caught Jerry Lee on television on *Shindig!* and the image became indelible. "When I create Jerry Lee Lewis in my mind, I see the eyes and the hair, and then you build out from that. His hair was worn the way certain guys in the area where I grew up — guys who were known as 'Hard Guys' — wore their hair. But those eyes, they were like a rattlesnake's. They see things through heat."

The 1950s, Alvin reflects, was a time of change on many unconscious levels. "The images that Jerry Lee, and Elvis, and a lot of those rockabilly guys represented, their personalities, were part of what was going on against conformity, racially and sexually. They were representing things that were happening, but they didn't know that they were representing things to society. The Fifties were when poor people could afford electricity, and they could afford electric instruments. The working class music merged, so blues and gospel and honky-tonk all merged to make this volcano, and all this energy and excitement and anger and joy and all that stuff that was in the working class community could burst forth in this big scream." He adds, "folk music went electric even before Bob Dylan did it at

Newport. And the Blasters based our sound around the Fifties stuff — r&b, and rockabilly, and blues — because that was when a poor guy could go get a cheap amp, turn it up real loud, and make a big noise."

Late-Seventies punks made a lot of noise, and though the Blasters weren't identified with the punk scene like X was, Alvin's band drew inspiration from the same sources. "Sun Records, because of Sam Phillips' attitude and philosophy towards recording, was based on a certain *anarchy*, and ours was too. I think the thing about Jerry Lee that attracted us, besides the image, was a certain intensity in his performances, as evidenced by the Star-Club record, that was appropriate for the time." The Blasters would play on the same bill as hardcore punk band Black Flag, streaking through "High School Confidential," "Breathless," and other Jerry Lee tunes via Hamburg, running the late-Seventies' unruly energy through the Killer's ageless attitude of reckless cool. "I'm all for balance in life," Alvin says, "but things had gotten to a point in popular music where they'd sort of de-fanged the coyote. The culture wars that went on; things got too polite. By going back to Jerry Lee, that was a way of us saying, "Enough of that, let's balance it out!" There was a lot of pent-up energy and emotion and anger in that era in society, and I think that rock & roll had gotten so far away from its Star-Club roots that it had to be kind of brought back to that."

Sometime before starting the Blasters, Alvin came across a Phillips import release of *"Live" At The Star-Club*, and the album became — as it would for Doe — a touchstone. "I have to say, the first time I listened to the album all the way through I was exhausted. There are so many emotions on the record. On the one hand it's a pretty aggressive record, but on the other hand — if you take in the whole back story, here's a guy that was a star, went back to nowhere — the album really captures him fighting it out. It also captures him going to where the audience doesn't care if he was shtupping his second cousin. He could be himself. He was liberated. And he was still physical enough, young enough, to take that approach to making music to its logical conclusion. He tears it down to its basics. He's got his demons — make a long list of Jerry Lee's demons — and he's fighting 'em, and there's anger there, and disappointment, and joy and release."

He adds, "Where I grew up, for me and the people I knew, the Stooges and the MC5, as great and as legendary as all those bands were, they just weren't part of my reality. It was music like *'Live' At The Star-Club* that was. When you're younger you have all of these silly conversations: 'What's the best Fuck You record of all time?' Was it Lou Reed's *Metal Machine Music*? I'd say, no, it was *Self Portrait* by Bob Dylan. Well, so is *'Live' At The Star Club*. The way I think about it is you've got a wolf that's caught in a trap, and Jerry Lee at the Star-Club is the sound of a wolf biting its own leg off."

A feral sound echoing across the decades. Jim Heath — more popularly known as the Reverend Horton Heat — has been testifying to rock & roll in venues large and small since the late 1980s, piling up long shows and longer miles with his trio in the name of what the Killer has sanctified. Heath's perspective is hard-earned. "Jerry Lee's music was wild, crazy, fast, and featured pounding straight eighth notes," he marvels. "After the mid-Sixties, music writers resorted to referring to any type of watered-down, psychedelic folk as 'rock & roll.' By the late Sixties, no popular music featured the rock & roll beat. It's sad, really. Music writers focused so much on the rock & roll attitude — of course, Jerry Lee had the attitude in spades, but that's not my point — that they forgot that the so-called rock & roll bands they loved in the late Sixties and on weren't rock & roll at all." Heath continues, "Look, rock & roll is Jerry Lee Lewis pounding straight eighths, not the Mamas and the Papas singing 'California Dreamin'. Rock & roll is Jerry Lee Lewis building and building every 12-bar pattern, not the Beatles singing 'Hey Jude'.

"I personally believe that in the centuries ahead, people will stop believing the crap that music writers say," Heath argues. "To them, rock & roll won't be Styx, Queen, Nirvana, Elton John, the Rolling Stones, or even AC/DC — it'll be Jerry Lee Lewis. I know this will piss off AC/DC fans especially, but 'Highway To Hell,' 'Dirty Deeds Done Dirt Cheap,' or 'T.N.T.' are not as fast as Jerry Lee's 'Whole Lotta Shakin' Goin' On,' which is about the slowest of his rock & roll beats. Okay, 'Whole Lotta Rosie' by AC/DC is maybe a little bit faster than 'Whole Lotta Shakin' Goin' On,' but it's still slower than all of Jerry Lee's other rock & roll beats. All of this is why during my shows, I announce, 'There are some country piano players who are more rock & roll than these big-haired, eye-liner-wearing, skinny-jeaned guys with giant Marshall amplifier stacks.'"

As Heath's ears have it, "Live" At The Star-Club proves that as late as the mid-Sixties Jerry Lee had everyone beat in the energy department. "Again, pounding straight eighths and non-stop boogie-woogie is what real rock & roll is all about," Heath says. "Jerry Lee always performed as if he had something to prove. It's nice that a simple, kind of tinny-sounding recording of Jerry Lee Lewis is holding up as a classic — twenty, thirty, and forty years after being overlooked by music industry insiders and critics of the day."

Heath adds: "'Thirty Nine and Holding' is one of my favorite country songs. It's funny to think that a rock & roller is more country than most country artists."

Sometimes I fantasize about what might have happened had Jerry Lee been energized by punk and New Wave, checked his ego, and given himself over to the likes of Nick Lowe and Dave Edmunds. The two hard-drinking Chuck Berry advocates could have provided Jerry Lee with as much bourbon as he wanted, respectfully discouraged him from re-recording his old hits, written and/or drummed up a stack of great songs, and backed him with the fantastic pub rock band Rockpile. Would the Killer have made a rockin' album that cashed in on the roots revivals of the late 1970s and early 1980s, or would he have churned out a lame effort, cursed by his stubbornness and his cranky inability to see beyond himself?

There are legions of die-hard rock & roll fans who don't listen to country music, and vice versa; like Johnny Cash, Jerry Lee remains legendary to both camps even if those camps don't overlap all that often. Critic Dave Marsh notes that pop radio historically has resisted country-crossover more than r&b-crossover, "which makes for one of contemporary culture's more interesting puzzles. Blacks are at all acceptable of course, because the black entertainer fulfills even the bigot's stereotype. But the white working-class music that makes up country remains a regional taste." In Jerry Lee's case, Marsh can't help but feel that that old warhorse "moral retribution" had a lot to do with the Killer's virtual disappearance from the pop charts after the 1950s.

Ultimately, what this amounts to is the anxiety of

classification. There are, of course, others who've muddied up the "River Category" more than Jerry Lee: Steve Earle, Dwight Yoakam, Emmylou Harris, Lucinda Williams, Willie Nelson, Gram Parsons, Jason Ringenberg, Robbie Fulks, Uncle Tupelo, Wilco, John Prine, Lyle Lovett, k.d. lang, Drive-By Truckers, Alejandro Escovedo, the Old 97s, Townes Van Zandt — to cite but a small number of country-infused artists who've successfully resisted labels that might consign them to one bin, one category, or the other.

But Jerry Lee Lewis remains inimitable. I'm at the end of this book and I still can't conjure a synonym for *unique* or *matchless* that isn't brutally weathered with overuse. The category in which Jerry Lee Lewis truly belongs is "Jerry Lee Lewis." The Killer is as big as Mount Rushmore, and he's also as American, as revered, as clichéd, as misunderstood, as corny, and as taken for granted as that monument. The curse of iconoclastic American success. Elvis felt it, so does Dylan. So will others who haven't been born yet.

"I'm always right," Jerry Lee Lewis once infamously said. "Once I thought I was wrong but I checked it out — I was right."

That's the Killer, that's funny. And it's half-true. Jerry Lee Lewis has been wrong many times. His surefire instincts — dwelling as they are within a wholly original and mercurial genius — have often led him astray in his career, and in his private life. As sound and artistic expression, "Breathless" from *The Golden Rock Hits Of Jerry Lee Lewis* is certainly wrong, just as "Your Cheatin' Heart" from *"Live" At The Star-Club* is certainly right. The Killer will keep going, keep singing, keep playing, until the

Maker Whom he's long feared and challenged shadows his ranch in hilly Mississippi and tells him that he's no longer right for this world.

SOURCES

A great pleasure in writing this book came from the time I spent with what others have written or said about Jerry Lee Lewis' songs, haunts, and myths; I gratefully acknowledge the work that preceded me. I'm especially obliged to the late Robert Palmer's personal, essayistic *Jerry Lee Lewis Rocks!*, among the first full-length books devoted to Jerry Lee, Nick Tosches' untouchable biography *Hellfire* and Myra Lewis' memoir *Great Balls Of Fire* — fascinating, accidental companion pieces published near each other — and Colin Escott's informative booklets that accompanied the Bear Family reissues in the mid-1980s.

Also helpful were Jimmy Gutterman's under-recognized *Rockin' My Life Away: Listening to Jerry Lee Lewis*, a lively and insightful journey through the Killer's catalogue, and Paul MacPhail's exhaustive *The Ferriday Fireball*, a day-by-day chronicle of Jerry Lee's public and private life. Among these books are strewn hundreds of articles, profiles and interviews, each intent with varying success on getting to the heart of the mystery of Jerry Lee's often stirring, often confounding music and life. I'm thankful to all of the writers — kindred spirits — whose work I used as helpful, duly-noted references, and as sound inspiration.

Regrettably, Jerry Lee Lewis declined my request for an interview for this book. Nashville Teens drummer Barrie Jenkins and guitarist John Allen did not respond to my repeated requests for interviews.

Interviews and Correspondence

Alvin, Dave. Email to the author. June 5, 2008.
—— Interview with the author. October 24, 2008.
Casson, Philip. Interview with the author. June 10, 2008.
Checksfield, Peter. Email to the author. August 6, 2008.
Corcoran, Michael. Email to the author. July 31, 2008.
Dickinson, Jim. Interview with the author. August 21, 2008.
Doe, John. Interview with the author. August 15, 2008.
—— Email to the author. August 16, 2008.
Duplock, Trevor. Email to the author. November 17, 2007.
—— Interview with the author. December 8, 2007.
—— Email to the author. December 9, 2007.
—— Email to the author. June 18, 2008.
Escott, Colin. Email to the author. July 14, 2008.
Fischer, Horst-Dieter. Email to the author. November 21, 2007.
—— Email to the author. January 8, 2008.
Flippo, Chet. Email to the author. August 23, 2008.
Hamp, Johnnie. Email to the author. June 9, 2008.
Harris, Pete. Email to the author. November 26, 2007.
—— Email to the author. June 19, 2008.
Hawken, John. Email to the author. November 12, 2007.
Heath, Jim. Email to the author. October 13, 2008.
Hills, John. Email to the author. June 19, 2008.
Hodges, Chas. Email to the author. March 9, 2009.
Inglott, Bill. Email to the author. November 11, 2007.
—— Email to the author. June 16, 2008.
Kennedy, Jerry. Interview with the author. July 25, 2008.
Knight, Graham. Interview with the author. June 7, 2008.
—— Email to the author. June 9, 2008.
—— Email to the author. June 10, 2008.
Loch, Siggi. Interview with the author. November 12, 2007.
—— Email to the author. June 18, 2008.
Lundgren, Ken. Email to the author. June 14, 2008.

—— Email to the author. June 28, 2008.

Malone, Bill C. Interview with the author. July 21, 2008.

Pennone, Pierre. Email to the author. November 17, 2007.

Singleton, Shelby. Email to the author. August 5, 2008.

Taylor, King Size. Email to the author. June 15, 2008.

Weize, Richard. Email to the author. January 9, 2008.

Books and Articles

Anonymous. "Program Slated for Friday." *The Daily Record, Stroudsburg-East Stroudsburg, PA*. May 1, 1958.

—— "Ferriday Sets Jerry Lee Lewis Day Saturday." *The Concordia Sentinel*. May 16, 1958.

—— "Knock the Rock." *The Morgantown Post*. June 10, 1958.

—— "Als er fertig war, kam . . . der Arzt!" *Musik Parade*. June, 1963.

—— "What a Fave Rave in 'Othello'!" Circa 1969. Reprinted in Escott, C. *The Killer: The Smash/Mercury Years, 1963–1968 of Jerry Lee Lewis. Vol. 1* (Bear Family, 1986).

Bernstein, Richard. "Memories of Hamburg, Enough to Build a Dream On." *New York Times*. April 8, 2006.

Berry, Chuck. *Chuck Berry: The Autobiography* (Harmony, 1987).

Best, Pete, and Patrick Doncaster. *Beatle! The Pete Best Story* (Dell, 1985).

Cain, Robert. *Whole Lotta Shakin' Goin' On: Jerry Lee Lewis* (Dial, 1981).

Carr, Patrick. "Cash Comes Back." *Country Music*. December, 1976. Reprinted in *Ring of Fire: The Johnny Cash Reader*. Michael Streissguth, ed. (Da Capo, 2002).

Clayson, Alan. *Hamburg: The Cradle of British Rock* (Sanctuary, 1997).

Connolly, Ray. "Great Balls of Scandal: How Jerry Lee Lewis' Marriage to a 13-year-old Wrecked His Career." *The Daily Mail*. May 24, 2008.

Doggett, Peter. *Are You Ready for the Country: Elvis, Dylan, Parsons and the Roots of Country Rock* (Penguin, 2000).

Duplock, T. "The Star-Club. Hamburg. April 5th, 1964." Personal reminiscence (unpublished).

Escott, C. *The Killer: The Smash/Mercury Years, 1963–1968 of Jerry Lee Lewis. Vol. 1* (Bear Family, 1986).

—— *The Killer: The Smash/Mercury Years, 1969–1972 of Jerry Lee Lewis. Vol. 2* (Bear Family, 1986).

—— *The Killer: The Smash/Mercury Years, 1973–1977 of Jerry Lee Lewis. Vol. 3* (Bear Family, 1987).

—— *Lost Highway: The True Story of Country Music* (Smithsonian, 2003).

—— *The Grand Ole Opry: The Making of an American Icon* (Center Street, 2006).

—— with Martin Hawkins. *Good Rockin' Tonight: Sun Records and the Birth of Rock 'n' Roll* (St. Martin's, 1991).

Fascher, Horst. *Let the Good Times Roll* (Eichborn Verlag, 2006).

Fischer, H.-D. "Jerry Lee Lewis at the Star-Club." *The Teenage Letter*. No. 3, 1964.

—— Personal reminiscence. (unpublished).

—— and Klaus Möbus. *Shaking Keyboard*. No. 18, 1964.

Floyd, John. *Sun Records: An Oral History*. Dave Marsh, ed. (Avon, 1998).

Gordon, Robert. *It Came From Memphis* (Faber & Faber, 1995).

Gould, Jonathan. *Can't Buy Me Love: The Beatles, Britain, and America* (Harmony, 2007).

Green, Richard. "Welcome To Jerry Lee Lewis Again." *New Musical Express*. March 20, 1964.

—— "Jerry Lee: Sensation." *New Musical Express*. March 27, 1964.

—— "Jerry Lee Lewis Comments on British Versions of the Tunes That He Made Famous First!" *New Musical Express*. April 4, 1964.

Guralnick, Peter. *Lost Highway: Journeys and Arrivals of American Musicians* (Perennial Library, 1989).

Gutterman, Jimmy. *Rockin' My Life Away: Listening To Jerry Lee Lewis* (Rutledge Hill, 1991).

Jarman, Rufus. "Country Music Goes to Town." *Nation's Business*. No. 41, February, 1953. Reprinted in Oermann, R. *A Century of Country: An Illustrated History of Country Music* (TV Books Inc, 1999).

Kaye, Elizabeth. "Sam Phillips." *The Rolling Stone Interviews: The 1980s*. Sid Holt, ed. (St. Martin's/*Rolling Stone*, 1989).

Kent, Nick. "The Killer in Aspic." *The Dark Stuff: Selected Writings on Rock Music 1972–1995* (Da Capo, 1995).

Kingsbury, Paul, ed. *The Encyclopedia of Country Music* (Oxford, 1998).

Knight, G. "I Remember the 1963 U.K. Tour." Personal reminiscence (unpublished).

—— "Jerry Lee Happenings: 1962–1966." Personal reminiscence. (unpublished).

Kreyling, Christine. "Reading the Row." *Reading Country Music: Steel Guitars, Opry Stars, and Honky-Tonk Bars*. Cecelia Tichi, ed. (Duke, 1998).

Lee, Denny. "36 Hours in Hamburg." *New York Times*. October 7, 2007.

Leigh, Spencer. *Twist and Shout: Merseybeat, The Cavern, The Star-Club, and The Beatles* (Nirvana, 2004).

Lewis, Jerry Lee. "Jerry Lee Lewis Writes About that Fantastic Tour — I Had a Ball and I'll be Back in October." *U.K. Disc Magazine*. May 26, 1962.

—— and Charles White. *Killer!* (Century Limited, 1993).

Lewis, Myra, with Murray Silver. *Great Balls Of Fire: The Uncensored Story of Jerry Lee Lewis* (Morrow & Company, 1982).

Lewisohn, Mark. *The Complete Beatles Chronicle* (Pyramid, 1992).

MacPhail, Paul. *The Ferriday Fireball: Jerry Lee Lewis* (self-published, updated periodically).

Malone, B. *Country Music U.S.A.* 2nd revised ed. (Texas, 2002).

Marcus, Greil. *Mystery Train: Images of America in Rock 'n' Roll Music.* 3rd revised ed. (Dutton Obelisk, 1990).

—— *The Dustbin of History* (Harvard, 1995).

Marsh, Dave. *The Heart of Rock & Soul: The 1,001 Greatest Singles Ever Made* (New American, 1989).

Middlebrook, Martin. *The Battle of Hamburg: Allied Bomber Forces against a German City in 1943* (Allen Lane/Penguin, 1980).

Millard, Bob. *Country Music: 70 Years of America's Favorite Music* (Harper Perennial, 1993).

Nite, Norm N. *Rock On Almanac: The First Four Decades of Rock 'n' Roll* (Perennial Library, 1989).

O'Connor, Flannery. "On Her Own Work." *Mystery and Manners* (Farrar, Straus and Giroux, 1969).

Oermann, Robert. *A Century of Country: An Illustrated History of Country Music* (TV Books Inc, 1999).

Palmer, Robert. *Jerry Lee Lewis Rocks!* (Delilah, 1981).

Pareles, Jon. "Weathered but Scrappy, Jerry Lee Lewis Rocks On." *New York Times.* September 28, 2006.

Pegg, Bruce. *Brown Eyed Handsome Man: The Life and Hard Times of Chuck Berry* (Routledge, 2002).

Roberts, Chris. "Jerry Lee Hits Britain." *Melody Maker.* March, 1964.

Schmemann, Serge. "Hamburg Journal: A Red-Light District Loses Its Allure." *New York Times.* May 14, 1988.

Sillescu, Werner. "Der Krawall ist harmloss und findet jetzt im Saale statt." *Hamburger Abendblatt.* May 29, 1963.

Stinton, Alan. "Jerry Lee Lewis Show Review." *The Record Mirror.* May, 1963.

Tosches, Nick. *Hellfire: The Jerry Lee Lewis Story* (Delacorte, 1982).

—— *Country: Living Legends and Dying Metaphors in America's Biggest Music.* Revised ed. (Scribner's, 1985).

—— *Where Dead Voices Gather* (Little, Brown, 2001).

Triplett, William. "Hamburgmania: On a Beatles Tour, the Old Haunts Still Rock." *Washington Post.* May 11, 2003.

Tucker, Stephen R. "Pentecostalism and Popular Culture in the South: A Study of Four Musicians." *Journal of Popular Culture.* Vol. 16, No. 3, Winter 1982.

Whitburn, Joel. *Billboard's Top 100 Charts: A Week by Week History of the Hot 100, 1958–1988* (Record Research, 1988).

—— *Billboard Pop Album Charts 1965–1969* (Record Research, 1993).

—— *The Billboard Book of Top 40 Albums.* 3rd ed. (Billboard, 1995).
—— *Joel Whitburn's Top Country Singles* (Record Research, 2002).
White, George R. *Bo Diddley: Living Legend* (Sanctuary, 1998).

Online

The American Club of Hamburg, e.V. www.americanclub.de/ACaboutHam.htm

"Box office/business for *American Graffiti*." IMDb.com. www.imdb.com/title/tt0069704/business

"American Milestones (Merle Haggard, Marty Robbins)." About.com: Country Music. www.countrymusic.about.com/library/blam3.htm

"The Beatles." The Rock and Roll Hall of Fame and Museum. www.rockhall.com/inductee/the-beatles

Brightonbeat. www.brightonbeat.com/home.htm

Center of Beat. www.center-of-beat.com

Coda, Kub. "Your Cheatin' Heart." allmusic.com. www.allmusic.com/cg/amg.dll?p=amg&sql=33:dpfyxc8aldfe

The Complete Works of the Rolling Stones 1962–2009. 1964. http://nzentgraf.de/books/tcw/works1.htm.

Corcoran, Michael. "First recorded gospel pianist got her start in Austin." Austin360.com. March 1, 2007. www.austin360.com/music/content/music/stories/2007/02/3dranes.html

Eder, Bruce. "The Nashville Teens." allmusic.com. www.allmusic.com/cg/amg.dll?p=amg&sql=11:k9ftxqw5ldde

Erlewine, Stephen Thomas. "*'Live' at The Star Club, Hamburg* [Rhino]." allmusic.com. www.allmusic.com/cg/amg.dll?p=amg&sql=10:fbfexqu5ldke

Fricke, David. "Keith Richards Uncut." RollingStone.com. www.rollingstone.com/news/story/5934855/keith_richards_uncut

Hamburg Museum. www.hamburgmuseum.de/index.html

Hamburg Star-Club. www.starclub-hamburg.com

Handbook of Texas Online — Panther Hall. www.tshaonline.org/handbook/online/articles/PP/xdp1.html

"Inductee List." The Rock and Roll Hall of Fame and Museum. www.rockhall.com/inductees/inductee-list/

"Interview: Trevor Duplock of the Giants." TheMarqueeClub.net. www.themarqueeclub.net/interview-trevor-duplock

Jerry Lee Lewis. A Rockabilly Hall of Fame Presentation. www.rockabillyhall.com/JLL.html

Jerry Lee Lewis > Charts and Awards > Billboard Singles. allmusic.com www.allmusic.com/cg/amg.dll?p=amg&sql=11:giftxqe5ldde~T51

"Jerry Lee Lewis: Grand Ole Opry, January 20, 1973." www.jerry-lee-lewis.40s-50s.info/cds/opry.htm

Jerry Lee Lewis: Unofficial Fan Forum. www.topfreeforum.com/
jerryleelewis/

"Jerry Lee Lewis Home, Nesbit, Mississippi." Backroads of American
Music. www.backroadsofamericanmusic.com/archive/2007/10/04/
jerry-lee-lewis-home-nesbit-mississippi.aspx

Johnson, Michael. "White Trash Saturday Night." www.dixie-chicks.
com/rockzilla/rockzilla3.html

Mersey Beat — Merseyside's Own Entertainment Paper. www.
triumphpc.com/mersey-beat/

Milo, Miles. "*Live at The Star Club, Hamburg* [Bear Family]."
RollingStone.com www.rollingstone.com/reviews/album/284513/
review/5940644/liveatthestarclubhamburg1964

"Nashville Cats: Jerry Kennedy." Country Music Hall of Fame and
Museum. www.countrymusichalloffame.com/site/experience-
events-detail.aspx?cid=2351

The Nashville Teens. www.nashville-teens.com/

Nielsen Ratings 1975–1980. www.angelfire.com/ny2/televisioncity/
7580.html

Planer, Lindsay. "*I Want Candy: The Best of the Strangeloves*." allmusic.
com. www.allmusic.com/cg/amg.dll?p=amg&sql=10:h9fuxqthld6e

Reeperbahn Hamburg Germany — Travel. www.travel-carhire.com/
reeperbahn-hamburg-germany.html

Sendra, Tim. "*'Live' Full House*." allmusic.com www.allmusic.com/cg/
amg.dll?p=amg&sql=10:3ifexqu5ldhe

Star-Club. List of beverages, circa 1964. Beatles Shop. www.beatles
shop.de/Bilder/Star-Club/GETRKARTE_65.JPG

Liner Notes

Anonymous. *Bo Diddley's Beach Party* (Pye, 1964).

Davis, Hank. *Killer: The Mercury Years, Vol. 1, 1963–1968* (Mercury,
1989).

Eder, B. *The Beatles Rockin' At The Star-Club in Hamburg, Germany,
1962* (Sony Music, 1991).

Fein, Art. *"Live" At The Star-Club, Hamburg* (Rhino, 1992).

Glass, Keith. *Another Place, Another Time/She Even Woke Me Up To
Say Goodbye* (Raven, 2002).

Kilroy, Eddie. *The Golden Rock Hits Of Jerry Lee Lewis* (Smash,
1964).

Lewis, Linda Gail. *In Loving Memories: The Jerry Lee Lewis Gospel
Album* (Mercury, 1971).

Lewis, Stuart. *Jerry Lee Lewis Sings The Country Music Hall Of Fame,
Vol. II* (Smash, 1969).

McRae, Andrew. *Country Songs for City Folks/Memphis Beat* (BGO,
2005).

Phillips, Colin. *"Live" At The Star-Club, Hamburg* (Phonogram, 1980).

Video

Jerry Lee Lewis: Greatest Live Performances of the '50s, '60s, and '70s (TimeLife DVD, 2007).

INDEX

Titles of albums, EPs, films and TV shows are in *italics*.

20 Rockin' Originals 6–9, 12–13, 50

AC/DC 189
"Act Naturally" 138
Albuquerque 33
"All The Good Is Gone" 150, 154
Allen, John 92, 94, 96, 103, 105,
    107–9, 111
Alvin
  Dave 119, 184, 186–8
  Phil 119
American Bandstand 20, 22, 40,
    134
American Federation of
    Musicians 32
American Graffiti 9–10, 12
American Hot Wax 10
Anderson, Bill 177
Animals, the 65, 72, 117
Anita Kerr Singers 39
"Another Hand Shakin'
    Goodbye" 171
"Another Place, Another
    Time" 150–2, 177
Another Place, Another Time 153,
    156–7
Arden, Don 63–4, 92
Australia 22, 40

"Babe I'm Gonna Leave You" 120
"Baby, Hold Me Close" 135
Bailey, Michael 64
Bare, Bobby 140
"Be-Bop-A-Lula" 39

Beatles 54–5
  at Candlestick Park 130–1
  early recordings by 62, 72
  Lewis reviews record by 71–2
  live album by 76
  at Star-Club 86
  success in US 74
"Before The Next Teardrop
    Falls" 154
Berry, Chuck 8, 22–3, 34, 86, 90,
    110, 117, 133–4, 155, 160, 162,
    179, 190
"Betcha Gonna Like It" 142–3
Big Beat 22–4, 61–2
"Big Blon' Baby" 40, 168
Big Bopper, the 7, 34
"Big Boss Man" 136
Big House 37
Birmingham Town Hall 72
Black Flag 187
Blackwell, Otis 62
Blasters, the 119, 184, 186–7
Blendells, the 135
"Blue Suede Shoes" 156
Bo Diddley 77, 81, 86, 117, 160
Boogie Woogie Country Man 170,
    172, 178
Boston 23–4
Bowman, Ernie 43
Bradford, Janie 106
"Break Up" 35, 37
"Breathless" 9, 12–14, 19, 22, 35,
    50–1, 185, 191
Brown, J. W. 15–16, 102, 184

Brown, James 76, 179
Brown, Myra 15–21, 24–5, 27, 32, 42–3, 48, 134, 144, 150–1, 163
Brown, Ray 163
"Brown- Eyed Handsome Man" 162
Buttrey, Kenneth 154
By Request: More Of The Greatest Live Show On Earth 131–3, 142

"Cadillac Man" 36
Calhoun, Lee 166
California 21
cannabis 111
Can't Buy Me Love 72, 110
"Carry Me Back To Old Virginia" 46
Cash, Johnny 34, 43, 76, 130–1, 137, 139, 148, 171, 174, 182, 190
Casone, Frank 46–7, 60, 126
Casson, Philip 64–5, 68–9, 71
Catch My Soul 150, 152
Charles, Ray 41, 59, 86, 108, 135, 179
Chess Records 76–7
Chestnut, Jerry 150, 154, 170
Chez Paree club 48
Chicago 7, 22, 47–8
Clark, Dick 7, 32, 40
Clayson, Alan 56, 86, 104
Clement, Jack 48, 135
"Cold, Cold Heart" 14
"Comin' Back For More" 168
Connolly, Ray 25–6
Cooke, Sam 179
"Cool, Cool Ways" 39
Corcoran, Michael 167
"Corrine Corrina 135
country music 137–8, 144–5
 Hall of Fame 181–2
 Outlaw tradition of 180, 182
Country Songs For City Folks 133, 137, 139–41
Cowtown Jamboree 130, 133–4
"Crazy Arms" 20, 141
Creedence Clearwater Revival 133
Cronkite, Walter 163
Crowe, Terry 120
"Cryin' Time" 132

"Damn Fine Country Song, A" 171
Dance Party 37
Davies, Gail 154
Davis, Oscar 33
Davis, W. D. 24
Dean, Jimmy 138
Demetrius, Claude 102
Denton, Bobby 149
"Detroit City" 140–1
Deutschlandhalle 84, 110, 117, 139
Dickinson, Jim 36–7, 167, 175–6, 182
Doe, John 184–6
Domino, Fats 21, 86, 90, 179
"Don't Let Go" 135
"Down The Line" 19, 96, 115–16
"Down Yonder" 177
Dranes, Arizona 167
"Dream Baby" 143
"Drinkin' Wine Spo-Dee-O-Dee" 28, 136
Dunford, Mick 120
Duplock, Trevor 97–100
Dylan, Bob 111, 158, 186, 188

Ed Sullivan Show, The 54
Eder, Bruce 118
Elektra Records 171–2
England 15, 21, 24–5, 34, 43–5, 63, 71–2, 84, 90, 92, 98, 110, 116, 120–1
Erlewine, Stephen Thomas 118
Escott, Colin 13, 50, 114, 127, 132, 171–2, 181
"Evening Gown" 173
Everly Brothers 86–7, 147, 179

Fascher, Horst 85
Feldman, Robert 61
Ferriday 22, 24, 37, 120, 164, 166
Fischer, Horst-Dieter 96–7, 101, 115
Flamin' Groovies 82–3
Flintstones 65–6, 93
Flippo, Chet ix, 181, 183
Floyd, John 41
"Folsom Prison Blues" 171
"Foolish Kind Of Man" 168
Fordyce, Keith 121
Freed, Alan 20, 22–3, 32, 40, 61

Frizzell, Lefty   130, 180

Georgia   21
Germany   44, 55–8, 60, 63, 75,
    92, 116
Giants, the   95, 97, 99–100
Gilley, Mickey   175
*The Golden Rock Hits of Jerry Lee
    Lewis*   49–50, 60, 113, 130, 191
Goldstein, Jerry   61
Good, Jack   152
"Good Golly Miss Molly"   97, 111
Gordon, Robert   182
Gordy, Berry   106
Gottehrer, Richard   61
Graceland   173
Grand Ole Opry   176, 181
Great Ball of Fire, The (EP)   20
"Great Balls Of Fire"   19, 35, 38,
    49, 65–6, 96, 111, 157, 185
Great Balls of Fire (film)   176, 184
Greatest Live Show On Earth, The
    127–30
"Green, Green Grass of
    Home"   138, 140
Green, Appends   73
Green, Richard   71, 101
Grosse Freiheit   59, 85, 101
*Gunfighter Ballads And Trail
    Songs*   139
Guralnick, Peter   180
Gutterman, Jimmy   41–3, 61, 63,
    100, 172

Haggard, Merle   136, 147, 154,
    158, 162, 180
"Hallelujah, I Love Her So"   136
Hamburg   54
    British bands playing in   92–3
    history of   55–9
    recording of "Live at the Star-
        Club"   2, 54
Hamp, Johnnie   64–5
"Hand Me Down My Walking
    Cane"   167
Happy Days   9–12
A Hard Day's Night   54, 109
Harman, Buddy   111, 154
"Harper Valley PTA"   142
Harrelson, Cecil   33–4, 43, 63,
    73, 164

Harris, Emmylou   168, 191
Harris, Pete Shannon   92–3, 95–6,
    103, 107, 112
Harrison, George   54, 109
Hawaii   21–2, 40, 76
Hawken, John   92, 117
Hawkins, Herman "Hawk"   128
"He Looked Beyond My
    Fault"   165
"He Took It Like a Man"   142
Heath, Jim   188–90
Hee Haw   137, 145, 156
"Help Me Make It Through The
    Night"   171
Hernando, Mississippi   19
"Hi-Heel Sneakers"   96, 121–2,
    129, 136
"High School Confidential"   24,
    34–5, 49, 67, 96, 105–6, 113,
    119, 187
Hills, John   98–9
"Hit the Road, Jack"   59–60, 152
Hodges, Chas   45
"Hole He Said He'd Dig For Me,
    The"   126–7
Holly, Buddy   22, 34, 179
"Home Away From Home"   170
"Hound Dog"   97, 104, 112
Howard, Harlan   157
Hutcheson, James Albert
    "Buck"   128

"I Believe In You"   135
"I Can Still Hear The Music In The
    Restroom"   171
"I Can't Seem To Say
    Goodbye"   177
"I Was Sorta Wonderin'"   171
"I Wish I Was Eighteen
    Again"   172
"I'd Do It All Again"   172, 174
Iggy Pop   39, 80, 184
"I'll Fly Away"   164, 166–7
"I'll Make It All Up To You"   14
"I'll Sail My Ship Alone"   38,
    132
"I'm A Lonesome Fugitive"   154
"I'm In The Gloryland Way"   168
"I'm On Fire"   61–3, 68, 115
"I'm So Lonesome I Could
    Cry"   177

In Loving Memories: The Jerry Lee Lewis Gospel Album   164–5
Inglott, Bill   91
"Invitation To Your Party"   160
"It Hurts Me So"   38
"It's A Hang Up, Baby"   143

Jackson, Wanda   130
Jagger, Mick   79, 118, 173
Janes, Roland   28–9, 41, 102
Jarman, Rufus   182
Jefferson Airplane   131
Jenkins, Barrie   92–4, 96, 102–3, 105, 107–9, 111, 117
Jennings, Waylon   180, 182
"Jenny, Jenny"   128
Jerry Lee Lewis Day   24
"Jesus Is On The Mainline"   171
"Johnny B. Goode"   135
Jolson, Al   37
Jones
  George   130, 146
  Tom   138, 140, 143
"Just Because"   136
"Just Dropped In (To See What Condition My Condition Was In)"   143

Kansas City   22, 33
"Kansas City" (song)   8
"Keep Your Hands Off It/Birthday Cake"   39
Kennedy, Jerry   47, 49, 59, 68, 128, 140, 142, 148–9, 152–3, 157, 159, 181
Kennedy, John F.   136
Killer Country   171–2
Kilroy, Eddie   50, 149–52
"King Of The Road"   141
King Size Taylor & the Dominoes   84, 86, 95, 99
KISS   76, 81
Knight, Graham   73
Koda, Cub   113
Krampre, Peter   90, 95, 97
Kreyling, Christine   182
Kristofferson, Kris   137, 158, 161–2, 171, 180
Kuykendall, Bill   130

"La La La La La"   135

Las Vegas   41, 46, 126, 161
Last Man Standing   172–3
Lee, Denny   57
Lennon, John   109, 118, 160
Lester, Richard   54
"Let a Soldier Drink"   152
"Let's Talk About Us"   158
Lewis, Frankie Jean   17
Lewis, Jane   19, 22
Lewis, Jaren   168, 175
Lewis, Jerry Lee
  1958 UK tour   25–6, 32
  1963–4 recordings   59–62
  1963 European tour   43–6
  1964 tour   63, 72–4, 84–5, 94–5, 119–21
  in 1970s   163–4, 168–9, 173–5
  1970s recordings   164–71
  alcohol and drug abuse   2, 14, 43, 96, 101, 159, 163, 169, 171, 173–4
  attitude to life   31–2
  autobiography   21, 46, 149, 169, 179
  commercial problems in US   32–3, 38, 42, 59–60, 62–3, 74–5
  divorce from Jane   22
  early career of   19–21, 35
  early recordings   113–14, 159–60
  at Grand Ole Opry   176–7
  on *The Greatest Live Show On Earth*   128–9
  greatest music of   1–2
  home life of   134, 144
  influences of   37
  late recordings   171–3
  later life   174–6
  leaving Sun Records   46
  on *"Live" at the Star-Club*   100–9, 111–14, 117–19, 184
  marriage to Myra Brown   14–16, 18, 20, 24
  meeting Myra Brown   16–18
  misconceptions about   9–10, 18–19
  musical gifts of   39
  musical signatures of   167–8
  in *Othello*   151–2
  performance on "Lewis Boogie"   28–30

post-scandal performances
    by   40–1
post-scandal recordings
    of   34–5, 39–42
post-Star Club recordings
    126–37, 139–43, 153–5,
    158–62
post-Star Club touring   142,
    144, 155–6
press reactions to   25–6, 87–90
pushes piano into sea at
    Yorktown   21
re-recording "Breathless"   13–14
on Ready, Steady, Go!   121–3
recording of "Live" at the Star-
    Club   90–2, 96, 114–15
relationship with backing
    musicians   93–4
relationship with Sun
    Records   42–3
riot at Boston performance   23
in Rock and Roll Hall of
    Fame   179
rock legacy of   183–7, 189–92
signs with Mercury Records   14
sued by Casone   126
television appearances   37,
    63–71, 133–4, 156–7
unreleased recordings by   38–9
and African rhythm   36
and alcoholism   159
and country music   138, 149–51,
    156, 180–3
Lewis, Jerry Lee Jr.   165, 173
Lewis, Kerrie   175
Lewis, Linda Gail   141, 160, 164
Lewis, Mamie   163
Lewis, Myra, see Brown, Myra
Lewis, Phoebe   48, 175
Lewis, Shawn   175
Lewis, Steve   43
"Lewis Boogie"   28, 30, 97, 111,
    184
"Lincoln Limousine"   136
Little Richard   35–6, 62, 64, 86,
    111–12, 128, 160, 167, 179, 185
live albums   40, 59, 75–8, 80–4,
    96–7, 119, 127–8, 130, 133, 161
"Live" at the Star-Club   97, 100–9,
    111–19, 127, 129, 184–9, 191
Liverpool   73, 98, 109, 138

Loch, Siggi   2, 90–1, 96–7, 100,
    106, 111, 115–16, 118, 129
Lomax, John III   181
"Long Tall Sally"   62, 97, 112
Louisiana   16, 21, 36, 75, 120, 150,
    164, 167
"Louisiana Man"   158
Louvin, Charlie   130
"Love Letters In The Sand"   28
Lovelace, Ken   150, 165, 170
"Lovin' Up A Storm"   40
LSD   111, 130
Lundgren, Ken   45
"Lust of the Blood"   152

Malone, Bill   162, 183
Manchester   64, 67, 73
Mann Act   34, 110
Marcus, Greil   10, 12, 26
Marsh, Dave   190
"Matchbox"   97, 107
"Maybeline"   134
Mayer, Roger   92
MC5   40, 81, 100, 188
McCartney, Paul   54, 109, 118
McCoy, Charlie   153
McRae, Andrew   140–1
"Me And Bobby McGee"   161
"Mean Woman Blues"   96, 102–5,
    177
Memorial Auditorium,
    Birmingham, Alabama   127,
    129
Memphis
    Lewis and Brown family in   16
    Lewis' home in   21
    Lewis recording in   14, 34, 41
Memphis Beat   117, 133–7
Memphis Beats, the   128, 131, 160
Mercury Records   13–14, 47–50,
    74, 142, 149, 157, 163–5, 172
MGM Records   113
Middlebrook, Martin   55
Miles, Milo   118
Miller, Roger   161
Mississippi   19, 36
"Money (That's What I
    Want)"   39–40, 106, 113, 133
Moody Blues   118
"Mother, Queen Of My
    Hearts"   171

Mullican, Moon 37–8, 132, 167
Murray "The K" 42
"My Boyfriend's Back" 61
"My Only Claim To Fame" 162

"Nadine" 110
Nashville 9, 13–14, 39, 48, 61, 144, 146–50, 157, 181–2
Nashville Teens
  experience in Hamburg 92–3
  on *"Live" at the Star-Club* 2, 103, 105–8, 111–12, 114, 117, 184
  post-Lewis career of 117–18
  supporting Lewis on tour 63, 84, 92–5, 97, 101
Natchez 16
Nelson, Willie 130, 180, 191
New Orleans 29, 35–6, 137
New York City 21, 42, 135
Nichols, Larry 128
"No Particular Place To Go" 110
"North To Alaska" 141

O'Connor, Flannery 176
Odd Man In 170–2
Ohio 22, 80, 147–8
"Old Rugged Cross, The" 165
"Old Time Religion" 28
"On The Back Row" 154
"On The Jericho Road" 166
"Once More With Feeling" 161–2, 177
"One Minute Past Eternity" 160
"One More Time" 170
Ono, Yoko 160
Orbison, Roy 34, 43, 102, 143
Outlaws, the 45
Over There (EP) 119
Owens
  Buck 129–32, 138
  Butch 173

Palmer, Earl 36
Palmer, Robert 35–6, 104, 144
Panther Hall 130, 132–3
Parton, Dolly 130
"Pen and Paper" 60, 152
Perkins, Carl 34, 107, 117, 148
Philips Records 68, 75, 90
Phillips, Jud 43

Phillips, Ray 92, 118
Phillips, Sam
  attempts to keep Lewis 46–7
  financial schemes with Frank Casone 126
  opinions of Lewis 30–1
  recording techniques of 36–7, 141, 187
  sale of Sun Records masters 13
Phillips Studio 41
Pickwick Records 7–8, 50
pills 2, 30, 75, 111, 122, 142, 144, 175
"Play Me A Song I Can Cry To" 154
Plebs, the 120, 122
Polydor Studio 115–16
Presley, Elvis
  in army 24, 34
  compared to Lewis 73
  cultural legacy of 186
  film career of 110
  leaving Sun Records 43
  Lewis' rivalry with 29
  version of "What'd I Say" 108
"Pumpin' Piano Rock" 28
Putnam, Claude 140

racism 11, 22
"Ramblin' Rose" 40
Ramones 78, 82, 100, 154, 184–5
Ready, Steady, Go! 120–1, 129
"Real Wild Child" 39
Reeperbahn 54, 57–9, 67, 85–8, 94–5, 98–9, 106, 110, 120
"Return Of Jerry Lee, The" 27–8, 30
Return of Rock, The 133–5
Reverend Horton Heat, *see* Heath, Jim
Rich, Charlie 34, 129, 148
Richards, Keith 76, 79, 172
Riley, Billy 37
Rivers, Jerry 154
Robbins, Marty 139
"Rock Around The Clock" 177
Rodgers, Jimmie 37, 162, 171, 180
"Roll Over Beethoven" 135
Rolling Stones 72, 76, 78–80, 110, 118, 131, 137, 173, 189

"Sexy Ways"   134
Sharp, Arthur   92
Shaver, Billy Joe   180
"She Even Woke Me Up To Say
   Goodbye"   158
*She Even Woke Me Up To Say
   Goodbye*   161–3
"She Still Comes Around (To Love
   What's Left Of Me)"   157
*She Still Comes Around (To Love
   What's Left Of Me)*   158–9
"She Was My Baby (He Was My
   Friend)"   126–7
Sheridan, Tony   71, 86
Shindig!   126, 134, 138, 186
"Shotgun Man"   143
Sillescu, Werner   87
Silverstein, Shel   161
sincerity   1–3, 127, 162, 182–3
Singleton, Shelby   13, 47, 50, 59,
   68, 74, 84, 127, 129–30, 135,
   141–3, 159–60, 181
"Sixty Minute Man"   39
"Skid Row"   136
Smash Records   13, 48–9, 119, 127,
   129–30, 133–5, 137–41, 152–3,
   156, 160, 163
Soul My Way   142–3
St. Louis   22, 33
St. Pauli   57–9, 85–7, 95
Star-Club, Hamburg
   Beatles at   55
   founding of   85–6
   Lewis' 1963 show at   44–5, 87–9
   Lewis' 1964 show at   54–5, 94–7,
      99–100, 114
   uniqueness of   86–7
Star-Club Records   90
Starr, Ringo   54, 109, 138
Statler Brothers   158
Steve Allen Show   20
Stewart, Gary   176
"Sticks and Stones"   136
Stinton, Alan   45
Stooges, the   80, 184, 188
Strong, Barrett   106
Sun Records   19, 22, 27–8, 34, 42,
   47, 147, 172, 187
   attitude to Lewis' career   31
   Lewis' contract with   46–7
Sun studio   23, 28, 35–7, 41

Sutton, Glenn   153, 162
Swaggart, Jimmy   166, 169, 175
"Sweet Georgia Brown"   170
Swingin' Neckbreakers   136
"Swinging Doors"   136, 154
Swit, Loretta   6

Tarrant, Morris "Tarp"   128
Taylor, King Size   86, 95, 115–16
"Teenage Letter"   46
"That Kind Of Fool"   172
"That Lucky Old Sun"   38–9, 166
*There Must Be More To Love Than
   This*   169–70
"There Stands The Glass"   158–9
"Thirty-Nine and Holding"   171,
   190
"This Must Be The Place"   136
"To Make Love Sweeter For You"
   157–8
"Tobacco Road"   92–3, 117–18
"Today I Started Loving You
   Again"   158
"Together Again"   129
"Too Young"   136
Tosches, Nick   20, 110, 151, 166
"Touching Home"   171
"Treat Her Right"   143
Triplett, William   55
Tubb, Ernest   150, 155, 180
Tucker, Tommy   121
"Turn On Your Love Light"   142
"Twist and Shout"   58, 74, 96

"Urge, The"   136

Valens, Ritchie   34, 77
Van Eaton, Jimmy   28–9, 35–7,
   41, 102
Velvet Underground   111
Vickery, Mack   172
Vincent, Gene   34, 39, 64–5, 86,
   160, 185
Virginia   21, 182

Wagoner, Porter   130, 139–40
"Waiting For A Train"   162
"Walk Right In"   141
"Walking The Floor Over You"
   150
Waxahachie, Texas   16

"Wedding Bells"   142
Weissleder, Manfred   85, 91
"What'd I Say"   14, 42, 44, 96,
    107–9, 133, 177
"What's Made Milwaukee Famous
    (Has Made A Loser Out Of
    Me)"   153–4
Wheaton, Maryland   6
"When The Grass Grows Over Me"
    162
"When The Saints Go Marching
    In"   28
When Two Worlds Collide   172
Who, the   76, 78, 139
"Who Will The Next Fool Be"   129
*Whole Lotta Shakin'
    Goin' On* (television
    performance)   63–4, 66–7
"Whole Lotta Shakin' Goin' On"
  at Grand Ole Opry   177
  on The Greatest Live Show On
    Earth   128
  and Lewis' legacy   185
  on *"Live" at the Star-Club*   112,
    167
  re-recording of   48–9
  on *Ready, Steady, Go!*   122

as revolutionary statement   104
sales of   20, 35
television performance of   63,
    69–70
"Wild Side Of Life, The"   140
Williams, Hank   37, 49, 66, 69,
    113, 132, 148, 154, 180, 182–3
Wills, Bob   130
Winkler, Henry   10–11
"Wolverton Mountain"   141
Womack, Bobby   78–9
Wonder, Stevie   75–6
Wood, Del   177
"Workin' Man Blues"   162, 177
"Would You Take A Chance On Me"
    171

X   184–5

Yorktown   21
"You Win Again"   14, 19, 66, 96,
    115, 132
Youngblood   176
"Your Cheatin' Heart"   49, 69, 96,
    113–14, 151, 191

Zint, Gunter   58